# Introduction

The virtual world of cyberspace has set the promising stage for an ideal setting for an ideal play unfolding towards the future of business marketing. It draws the curtains open with reinvented marketing tools while programming its audiences to embrace the general outlook and spirit of the times — "The New Era of Social Media Marketing - 2018."

All the products presented therein are futuristic. Otherwise, a psychological countertransference or an illusory perspective, which arises in reaction to the emotions, experiences, or issues at hand, will simply adjust and correct them immediately. Experiential marketing will continue to engage customers and create for them a strong emotional attachment to a product or service.

In just a short time, engagement marketing or interactive experience marketing — the promotional strategy involving the creation of an interactive experience, which captures the attention of customers to not only compel them talking about your brand or product but also, to motivate them experimenting with and referring your brand to others — has rapidly become the frontline of business marketing campaigns.

The growing trend has been even entrenching firmly itself as an integral part of the lives of current and future generations. To state a simple fact, brands can now reach out easily and interact literally with its target audience sans shelling out the high costs usually associated with and required by traditional advertising practices.

More importantly, creating interactive campaign ideas requires you just about the same amount of time and effort as you would create a traditional PR campaign or advertising. Through interactive campaigns, your brands or products gain a boost in awareness, interest, demand, and calls-to-action that keep your audience yearning for more and engaged endlessly.

Nevertheless, with several creative campaign methods and techniques already available at present, the gargantuan challenge confronting brands is choosing the proper channels that can ably retain the engagement of the audience, no matter what.

According to veteran marketers, a couple of campaign models are revolving around today's interactive space. The first type deals practically with the augmented and virtual worlds; the second type enhances everything virtual with embedded strategies. Actually, any brand or product can apply easily either of these campaign models or both, to expand its reach.

During the recent past, audience engagement was indeed a pressing requirement. Yet, achieving even the slightest satisfactory outputs necessitates solutions of physical inputs, which were mostly a tiring and laborious affair. Nowadays, while the urgency of keeping an engaged audience remains, the solutions and tools available have become much easier and more convenient to collaborate with; thanks largely in part to the embedded techniques and interactive experiential campaigns.

The world of marketing has changed drastically from the rudimentary days of flashing a brand's logo just about everywhere to capture the attention of its audience. People are now wiser, much less, not easily persuaded to give in for a swift approval.

Instead, consumers had always wanted a direct connection with a real personality, for whom they are convinced perceiving as someone trying to help solve their problems. Inasmuch as possible, they wanted to relate their fondness, sentiments, and experiences with the brand, product, or service, and share it to the rest of humanity to partake in its pride, value, and goodwill.

The ivory tower of corporate marketing that has stood out imposingly during the earlier stages of marketing is certainly crumbling and fading away into oblivion. Building strong interpersonal connections and intimate networks between a company and its clientele has definitely become the new norm and marketing frontier — with unfilled threats and unfilled hopes — for which social media is augmenting to realize it all.

**Social media marketing (SMM), a typical mode of online or Internet marketing utilizes a host of social networking platforms as its principal marketing tool.** The objective of SMM is to produce digital contents, which users eventually share through their various social networks to assist a certain company boost its programs of brand awareness, exposure, interest, and demand while broadening its customer base and reach.

A key component in the practice of SMM is the application of social media optimization (SMO). **Similar to search engine optimization (SEO) that enhances the ranking of a web page or site in the search engine results page (SERP), SMO is a marketing strategy for drawing in unique and new visitors to a website.** You can implement SMO in a couple of ways: either promoting your activity by updating your tweets, statuses, or blog posts through different social media channels or, affixing social media links to contents, like sharing buttons and rich site summary (RSS) feeds.

SMM benefits a company by gaining direct feedback or reviews from its current customers, as well as potential leads. At the same time, any interactions transpiring from these customers' feedbacks transform the company to be seemingly more approachable and personable. The interactive elements of social media — termed collectively as social customer relationship management (social CRM) — ably provide customers the once elusive chance of feeling heard by voicing out whatever complaints or inquiring any pertinent questions to the company.

With the steadily growing popularity of social media networks, specifically Facebook, Twitter, Tumblr, Pinterest, Instagram, Flickr, YouTube, Vimeo, and LinkedIn, SMM has become a common and indispensable habit. As a response to SMM's importance to consumerism, the Federal Trade Commission (FTC) — America's leading consumer protection agency — has updated correspondingly its rules to accommodate SMM sector.

In FTC's May 2017 Endorsement Guides publication, it stated that whenever a company or its accredited advertising agency provides an online commenter or any blogger with free company products or complementary services or other forms of incentives for the generation of positive blurbs and promotional statements, FTC will be treating all these relative online comments as legal endorsements.

In this case, both the company and the blogger must be responsible for ensuring clear and transparent disclosures for the provision of the incentives. All posts of the blogger about the product or service shall contain no unsubstantiated or misleading statements, and otherwise, duly comply with the FTC's governing rules regarding deceptive or unfair advertising practices.

Essentially, a proper implementation of social media with your present marketing plan can foster an accelerated growth of your business with cost-effective support and resources. Nonetheless, not all social media outlets are suited for every nature or type of business. You ought to figure out the perfect match that will most truly help to reach out effectively and efficiently your customers.

This informative guidebook intends to present you with a comprehensive overview of the exponential powers that social media delivers to your marketing war room. It demonstrates the value and potentials of social media in experiential campaigns.

For anybody who has been into the marketing scene for quite some time now but still finds the concept of applying social media as an alien undertaking, this helpful manual will interlock the basic concepts of marketing with the amazing enigmas of social media.

For new marketers who are already in the thick of using social media but are still thinly informed and unsure of implementing the proper ways to attract customers and earn money, this fundamental SMM handbook will be guiding you in conveying your social media skills to the world of business.

Through learning and understanding the inherently unique capabilities of social media channels, you will be optimizing your marketing plans and efforts like never before. This book will be your blueprint to build and develop your social media empire!

*"You ought to develop a kinship of a loyal tribe and great devotees who simply want to listen to what you have to say."*

**— Roger Burns**

## Notarial Notes

The contents presented herein constitute the rights of the First Amendment.

All information states to be truthful, accurate, reliable, and consistent. Any liability, by way of inattention or otherwise, to any use or abuse of any policies, processes, or directions contained within, is the sole responsibility of the recipient reader.

The presentation of the entire information herein is without a contract or any form of guarantees or assurances. Therefore, any information hereupon solely offers for informative purposes only, and as such, universal.

The trademarks used herein, are without any consent. Thus, the publication of the trademark is without any permission or backing by the trademark owner/s.

All trademarks and brands mentioned within this book are for clarification purposes only and owned by the owners themselves, not affiliated with the author or publisher.

Thank you for supporting the rights of the author and publisher.

© Copyright 2018 by Green Raccoon Publishing

All Rights Reserved

In accordance with the U.S. Copyright Act of 1976, the reproduction, scanning, photocopying, recording, storing in retrieval systems, copying, transmitting, or circulating in any form by any means— electronic, mechanical, or otherwise— any part of this publication without a written permission from the publisher, constitutes piracy or theft of the author's intellectual property rights.

Exceptions only include cases of brief quotations embodied in critical reviews and/or other certain non-commercial uses permitted by copyright law. Alternatively, when using any material from this book other than reviewing simply, obtain prior permission by contacting the author.

Both author and publisher shall be, in no case, held liable for any fraud or fraudulent misrepresentations, monetary losses, damages, and liabilities— indirect, consequential, or special— arising from event/s beyond reasonable control, or relatively set out in this book.

If advice is necessary, consult a qualified professional for further questions concerning specific or critical matters on the subject.

## Table of Contents

**INTRODUCTION** — 1

**CHAPTER 1 – THE FUNDAMENTALS OF MARKETING** — 11

The Marketing Plan and Its Basic Anatomy ............... 12

Principal Processes of the Marketing Mix Theory: The Standard 8 Ps of Strategic Marketing ............... 19

**CHAPTER 2 – SOCIAL MEDIA AND MARKETING** — 25

The Basic Concept of Social Media Marketing ............... 28

    Definition of Social Media ............... 29

    Definition of Social Media Marketing ............... 31

    Importance of Social Media Marketing in Your Business ...... 34

**CHAPTER 3 – EFFECTS OF SMM ON CONSUMERS' PURCHASING RESPONSES: THE SOCIAL FEEDBACK CYCLE** — 36

Importance of Social Customer Service ............... 43

Learning Approach for Marketing Professionals about the Social Web ............... 45

E-Commerce Inbound Marketing ............... 48

**CHAPTER 4 – PURPOSES AND BENEFITS OF SOCIAL MEDIA MARKETING** — 52

Brand Awareness or Product/Service Exposure ............... 55

Demographic and Geographic Targeted Traffic ............... 60

Lead Generation and Conversion ............... 64

Market Research Insights and Competitor Analyses ............... 66

Social Customer Service, Consumer Interaction, and Feedbacks ............... 71

Cost-Effective Marketing Solution ............... 73

Public Relations and Social Recruitment System of Human Resources .................................................................................. 76

Summary of the Social Media Marketing Benefits for Businesses .................................................................................................. 78

**CHAPTER 5 – THE DIVERSE WORLD OF SOCIAL MEDIA NETWORKS  79**

Social Networks: The Primary Component of the Social Web...86

**CHAPTER 6 – SOCIAL AND BUSINESS NETWORKING SITES  88**

Facebook ................................................................................. 89

LinkedIn ................................................................................. 105

**CHAPTER 7 – BLOGGING AND MICRO-BLOGGING SITES  115**

Twitter ................................................................................... 119

Tumblr ................................................................................... 130

**CHAPTER 8 – SOCIAL MEDIA PHOTO AND VIDEO SHARING SITES  137**

Pinterest ................................................................................ 138

Instagram .............................................................................. 147

YouTube ................................................................................ 159

Vimeo .................................................................................... 168

Flickr ..................................................................................... 175

**CHAPTER 9 – BONUS. CREATING THE ESSENTIAL ELEMENTS OF YOUR IDEAL AND SYSTEMATIC SOCIAL MEDIA MARKETING PLAN  182**

Step 1 – Establish Your Social Media Marketing Objectives....183

Step 2 – Conduct a Comprehensive Survey and Audit of Your Current and Prospective Social Media Accounts ................... 185

Step 3 – Improve Your Social Media Profile Accounts: The Creation and Reinvention of Your Audience Persona ............ 187

Step 4: Collate Social Media Marketing Inspirations ................ 188

Step 5: Create Your Social Media Content Marketing Plan ..... 189

Step 6: Allocate Your Budget and Resources .......................... 191

Step 7: Test, Evaluate, and Adjust Your Strategy .................... 192

**SOCIAL MEDIA IS THE INTERNET: A CONCLUSION**    **195**

## Chapter 1 – The Fundamentals of Marketing

*"If you do not start in the right spot, you are going to lose the game before you even get started."*

**— Mike O'Neil**

Prior to plunging directly into the vast sea of marketing through social media, it would rather be prudent to avail a crash course about marketing by its general sense of the term. After all, marketing is, foremost, your extremely important business process to undertake in order to spur your business venture, or any enterprise for that matter, towards success.

Thus, what is marketing exactly all about? For a plain and simple understanding, marketing can be, as follows:

Marketing is the art of communicating and conveying a value proposition of a specific brand — either a product or a service — to a targeted audience. This mere definition of marketing should not pose that much of a strange concept for all of us. Most of the time in our lives, we always attempt at communicating and conveying value to our fellowmen!

When you began applying for a job, did you not try communicating the value you were supposed to impart to your potential employer? When you finally asked your better half to live under one roof, have you never tried convincing each other that living together would make your lives better and happier?

In these twin life-changing instances, both are no different from marketing a product or a service!

Indeed, marketing is very crucial in our lives since it enables people around us know of our existence and the reason why they should mind and care. When nobody knows who you are, you are essentially inexistent, invisible! Likewise, in the world of business, this similar notion holds true!

You may have the greatest and most useful widget ever created; yet, if you are not able to persuade and engage anybody of why there is an urgent need to purchase it, then your business is dead in the water. Nonetheless, before going out with your sales pitch and telling the whole world the reasons why your brand is an important necessity or the most indispensable item for them, you should need to develop primarily a solid, sustainable, and strategic marketing plan!

### The Marketing Plan and Its Basic Anatomy

Knowing exactly where you are going is the ideal path towards reaching your destination. Would you hop on a plane without even knowing where it will be landing? Perhaps, the adventurous spirit in you would get aboard without hesitation, but most people would always think and feel much safer knowing that they are going to land where they really intended. The same goes for your business endeavors.

When you are starting out in business, a couple of factors are oftentimes scarce, if not, indefinite and variable — resources and time. Thus, for you to create new and effective business strategies that ensure yourself not wasting your time, efforts, and funds, you truly need a fundamental marketing plan!

Your marketing plan is actually a request for resources in return for targeted or promised extents of incremental unit sales, revenues, and profits or market share. This means that you can always create and develop your respective marketing plans for brands, products, services, or market segments.

A strong and workable marketing plan allows you to see the panorama of your business orientation and directions. It shows you how each component of your plan will help you and your business arrive at your intended destination.

Just the simple act of rolling up your sleeves, sitting down, and forcibly thinking, anticipating, and focusing all the details of how you will operate your business and convey your message to your target customers will greatly help you avoid common mistakes and eventual pitfalls of doing business. While recording your plan in writing, you can even think of a thing or two to include in your strategy! There are times when you stumble upon serendipity or discover the missing link to the plan that you may never have had, had you not written down your marketing plan.

Yet, a lingering question remains. Would having a concrete and viable marketing plan denote that everything would be flowing smoothly? Definitely, it would not! You must take into account the unforeseen and fortuitous events, which are generally normal occurrences in life. You just have to address and resolve these natural issues to stay on course.

As conditions change, you must always revisit and update your plan to make the necessary and appropriate modifications. Possess the ideal quality of flexibility so that you can act better adapting to any unexpected events that may crop up.

Every marketing plan requires the property of being adaptable to fit the specific needs and natures of the market conditions and the business itself. Even so, the ideal marketing plan constitutes a standard anatomical outline of the barest elements, which you cannot simply do without, and with which to help you define clearly how you should retain a steady sales growth and manage effectively all the marketing aspects of your business.

Each component is crucial since it often interrelates to other elements of your plan. The following are basic summaries of the minimum essentials that should be in the pipeline of your marketing plan:

💻 Business Vision and Mission Statement – The heart and soul of your business is your mission statement. It is the main reason and the driving force that motivates you doing what you do. Besides, your business vision and mission statement will form the market's impression and proper perspectives about you and your business.

Generally, this marketing element is a single, well-articulated sentence that will compel readers with a desire to know more about the business. You can only summarize such statement after you have finally completed mapping out the entire plan.

💻 Sales Forecasts and Objectives – Your projections and goals are the cognitions of your business. Typically, these are in the form of detailed periodic forecasts. Their purpose is to evaluate your advancement of reaching your set goals and objectives (i.e., entice new leads, urge repeat and add-on purchases, incentivize trials, increase market share, modify value perception, improve emotional bonds, increase brand awareness and loyalty, extend towards novel products or services categories, etc.).

In addition, setting the sales forecasts and objectives of your business will serve as your groundwork for your marketing budget and cash flow. You can actually create sales forecasts for each product or product line for the market you cater for each location you serve and for each marketing channel you prefer.

💻. Marketing Budget and Cash Flow – Funds are the lifeblood of your business. Depending upon your sales forecasts and objectives, develop a monthly schedule of your planned marketing expenditures. This will also include defined metrics (i.e., financial projections, cash flows of executing the plan, balance sheets, pro forma profit and loss statements, etc.), which enable activating decision points or cautionary prompts of pausing the operations of the business if it falls substantially short of its return on investment (ROI).

Fundamentally, budgeting offers you to benchmark specific financial processes, particularly during the assessment of effective costs vis-à-vis estimated costs. Hence, you should have a detailed budget plan, which categorizes certain types of your marketing actions and activities.

💻 Market Research and Competitive Analysis – The backbone of your marketing plan is your gathered and collated data from the analytical and qualitative research of your market and the competition. On one hand, market research or an analysis of the market should include identifying any external market factors that can influence positively or negatively on your business. Specifically, this shall cover information about the market size, market trends and activities, distribution costs, and your target consumers (i.e., needs, insights and expectations, income bracket, etc.), as well as their purchasing habits.

On the other hand, the information about the competition shall include a strengths-weaknesses-opportunities-threats (SWOT) analysis, along with their strategies and positioning. In this case, you should know who your close competitors are and compare how their products or services differ from yours (i.e., pricing, market segment reach, etc.).

Knowing the ways and byways of your market and competitors will serve as your guide on how to stand out and be distinctive from the competition. This implies working out a better positioning and presentation of your business through further customer research (i.e., market test results, volumetric modeling, concept testing, qualitative research, etc.).

💻 Perception and Positioning – The status and appearance of your business in the marketplace significantly impart a lasting impression on your customers. The positioning of your business is the difference in how your specific target market perceives it.

For instance, if your restaurant business offers burgers as its house specialty, do patrons perceive your establishment as the right eating place for healthier burger options (e.g., vegan, low-sodium, gluten-free, high-calorie, less fat, etc.) or the best place to fill appetites for a double quarter pounder cheeseburger?

Hence, this leads you to develop a compelling brand messaging or a marketing strategy that communicates clearly or defines how you wanted your customers to perceive your business. It would be crucial for your business to have a solid unique selling proposition (USP) since this will certainly distinguish your outfit from your main competitors.

🖥 <u>Marketing Strategy</u> – The brighter path towards achieving your sales objectives is your marketing strategy. The core of your strategy is the response to how your business finds your customers, retains them, and attracts new leads and prospects.

The marketing strategy shall be looking at the entire situations of the marketplace. It is where your principal marketing strategies derive breaking down further explicit marketing tactics (i.e., direct mailing and e-mailing campaigns, couponing, sales and promotional events, social media, podcasts, digital content marketing strategy, street promotional teams, brochures/catalogs/flyers, newsletters, seminars/webinars, partnership programs, and other similar items or activities leading to gain direct access to customers and prospects).

The aforementioned methodologies and tactics must be touching upon all the essential elements of the marketing plan so that you will be able to perform properly the <u>principal processes of strategic marketing</u>. All these marketing processes align with your core business intents of creating brand awareness, generating interest, imposing a desire and demand, and enforcing a call-to-action of purchasing your products or availing your services.

🖥 <u>Evaluation Metrics</u> – You can determine the strengths and weaknesses of your marketing plan by evaluating your marketing activities and programs with certain metrics. One is using Google Analytics to monitor your marketing success in terms of website conversions. Another is using a simple spreadsheet to assess your marketing budget versus actual ROI.

Test your programs and evaluate their results over a defined period. You only have to repeat any programs delivering direct sales or sign-ups to your list of emails and rid those that are not.

🖳 [Risks and Contingency Plans]() – As mentioned, you can only evaluate your marketing plan depending on the corresponding results of its implementations. Thus, your plan must also include diversionary tactics and effective contingency measures to prepare for future risks and address such eventualities that derail your marketing strategies.

These contingent maneuverings involve designated people who will be responsible for specific activities. They must have corresponding working schedules with definite deadlines for the evaluation and revision processes of the marketing activities in your plan.

Bear in mind that whenever your business is not yielding or bringing in leads, then you and your business necessitate a rather more feasible and sound marketing plan that will always help you get started. If need be, start again from scratch! Nothing can beat a mapped plan that serves as the beacon light for navigating your business vessel appropriately towards the shores of success.

However, no matter how you and your people conducted greatly the market research process or how you have formatted and organized neatly all your documents, but you just never worked constantly upon implementing the essential actions of your marketing plan, then everything is simply a waste of your valuable resources and time.

Like any other business plans, marketing plans possess a similar critical aspect, which is the implementation stage. Without any action done, any plan becomes inutile and loses all its purposes. As always, plan and organize your work; work your organized plan!

## Principal Processes of the Marketing Mix Theory: The Standard 8 Ps of Strategic Marketing

**Strategic marketing is integral to your business planning processes.** The process of strategic marketing begins by identifying the needs of your customers, and thereby, creating the ideal marketing plan for achieving customer satisfaction, improving business performances, productivities, and profits.

Your regularly updated marketing plan, which supplies the references of your marketing actions, records details of all the results of your strategic marketing efforts. Foremost, it dictates what method of marketing programs that your business will be applying over a given period and how to implement those programs.

Stated alternatively, strategic marketing seeks out the establishment of a unified or streamlined purpose, as well as mapping out a clear direction for all your marketing campaigns. Nonetheless, its fundamental goal is to achieve a sustainable competitive edge.

For the realization of this ultimate goal, strategic marketing should meet the following required objectives:

💻 Set the primordial goal under the guidelines of the S.M.A.R.T. criteria for goal setting — Specific, Measurable, Attainable, Relevant, and Time-Based.

💻 Take into account the previous marketing failures and learn from their lessons to improve performance.

💻 Create and develop more effective and efficient business tactics.

💻 Identify the most significant ways that must alter the business operations.

Oftentimes, the bulk of your marketing materials and advertising messages — explicit marketing tactics — comprise the extensive usage of powerful calls-to-action. The basic design of such calls-to-action instructions is to demonstrate clearly to your customers how to take the next desired step and create a sense of necessity or urgency around what your business offers.

The bottom line is to render your consumers with obliging reasons to make a prompt purchase instead of deferring their purchasing decisions. **This is where strategic marketing gushes forth.**

In summary, strategic marketing is the method by which your business differentiates itself effectively from the rest of the competition. Accordingly, it takes advantage of its current and potential strengths to provide value to your customers more consistently and much better than what your competitors offer.

In principle, it would seem that everything is very simple. Yet, strategic marketing truly means much more than being creative, or adept at implementing the 'marketing mix' theory.

The venerable theory of the marketing mix refers to the combination of factors or set of marketing tools that your business controls to pursue the marketing goal of influencing consumers to purchase your products or take your services.

Initially, the theory presents four broad aspects of a marketing decision focusing on product lines or selling a product, to wit: product, price, place of distribution, and promotion. However, for the strategic marketing of a business concentrating on providing services, it further includes details of productivity and quality, physical evidence, processes, and people or personnel.

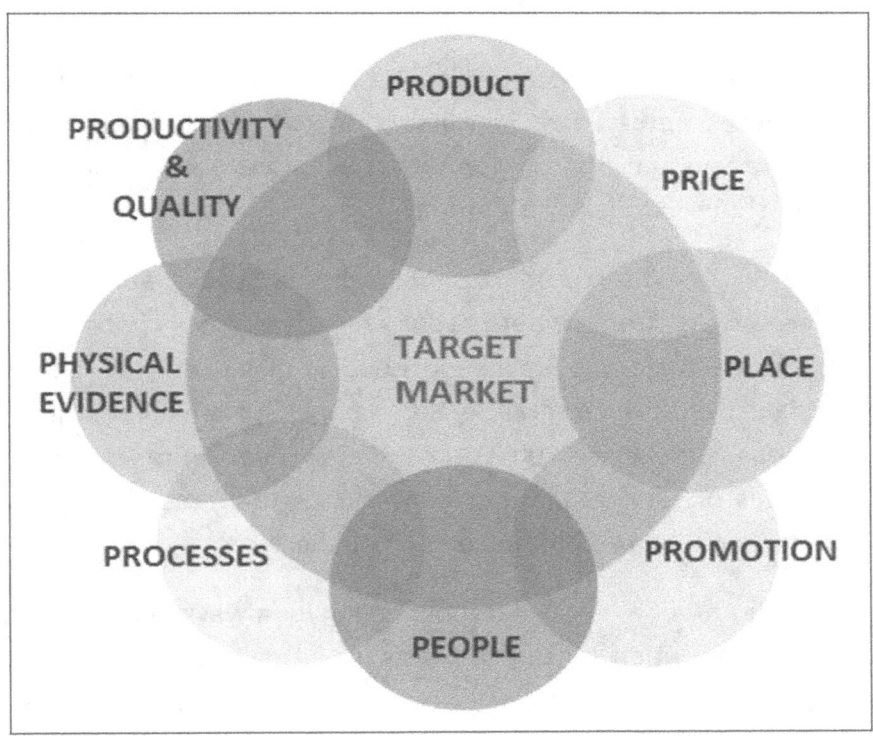

*Image - 1: Diagram of the Principal Processes of the Marketing Mix Theory In Relation To the Target Market*

🖥 Product – Your product should always be tailor-made for the needs and wants of the consumers. It must not only satisfy requirements of function (or fashion) but also, match the discriminating tastes and meet the high expectations of your target market.

Take good care of your product; it is everything you got. Your business is your product, and your product is your business.

🖥 Price – Your product should always impart positive perceptions that it exemplifies good value for money. However, pricing must not muddle with the consumer's mindset that your product is the cheapest available on the market.

On the contrary, note well that a principal doctrine in marketing concepts attests that consumers do not usually mind to pay an extra amount for an item that is more than beneficial and functions excellently for them.

🖥 Place – Your product should always be available and easily accessible from where your target market finds it most convenient to shop. Your distribution places may be either the high street (urban retail sector comprising of small or large stalls, shops, and service outlets) or the mail order route (purchasing of goods or services via mail delivery), or the latest social concept alternative via e-commerce or an online shop.

🖥 Promotion – Your product should always adopt a crucial communication tool in the form of either a sales promotion or public relations (PR), or personal or direct selling schemes, or multi-media advertising, or the more popular mode of customer engagement in recent times — social media.

These marketing communication tools span the link between your external stakeholders— your customers — and your business outfit. Their chief purpose is to deliver across a bright message of your organization to your target audience in a manner they would preferably like to listen — be it plainly informative or earnestly appealing to their urgencies and emotions.

💻 Productivity & Quality – Your services should always offer your customer a great and fair deal. In this aspect, it speaks less about your business improving upon its productivity vis-à-vis cost management (or the processes of planning and controlling your budget), but more about how you deliver your improved productivity or quality services to your customers.

💻 Physical Evidence – Your services should always include some form of concrete elements albeit most of what your customer pays is intangible. For instance, a labor construction company would provide its client with a completed house. Another example would be an insurance outfit giving its customers printed documents of their contract or policy.

In certain cases where customers receive an online document like XPS files or PDFs, which is neither a physically printed nor a tangible material, these customers are still apparently receiving a physical product by the absolute definition of the term, physical evidence.

💻 Processes – Your services should always include processes of direct and indirect activities. The former adds value to your clients as you perform your services directly midst their presence. In this manner, how well you delivered your services manifests their experience, which is actually part of what your customer pays for.

The latter process of indirect activities, known as back-office activities, is usually a support mechanism activated before, during and after rendering your services. Essentially, processes entail inputs, throughputs, and outputs. Marketing is responsible for adding value to each of these stages.

Moreover, marketing has several of types of processes. A fine example trending at present are the electronic processes such as loyalty swipe cards, Electronic Point-Of-Sale (EPoS) and credit card payment systems, and product barcodes scanned not only by cashiers at the checkout line but also by customers using their smartphones.

🖥 People or Personnel – Your services should always be trusted performances rendered by the right and reliable people— from the frontline sales and customer service staffs all the way up to the managerial personnel. Your people are essentially as much a functioning element of your business offering as the services you are offering.

Although the original marketing mix theory has been in place since 1960 and undergone subsequent updates during the 1970s and 1980s, it endures remaining very much applicable and relevant in today's day-to-day work of marketers. Marketers rely on and adopt the sound logic of the theory's eight principal processes while facing the constant changes of the times, particularly in communication modalities such as social media.

> *"People relate to other people, not sales pitches and marketing jargons."*
>
> **— Janet Fouts**

# Chapter 2 – Social Media and Marketing

*"Social media marketing is about the people and not about your business. Provide for the people and the people will provide you."*

— **Matt Goulart**

In essence, humans are social animals. We love and urgently needed to interact and socialize with one another. Truly, interaction and communication are necessary elements for sustaining human society.

The dawn of Internet technology has altered drastically the manner by which people communicate. Either writing a letter via snail mail or booking an overseas telephone call, both are now simply antediluvian social mementos. Currently, technology allows anybody to link up instantaneously with family and friends across the seven seas.

Observe the social lifestyle of most people nowadays. Oftentimes, you see people spending more than a couple of hours each night on the Internet, chatting or communicating with friends and like-minded people. The Internet made socialization and making friends easier than ever.

With the Internet as a global phenomenon, folks of all ages from all over the world usually seek out social networking sites dealing with certain topics of their concerns and interests that could build social and business networks. They come and commune together at these sites to converse and share information, knowledge, and their insights, as well as following most of the conversations transpiring therein.

When speaking about social networking, we usually denote it to the chatting activities per se or those online forums and blogs where people discuss particular topics. The usage of social media actually goes beyond these usual communication activities.

Social media networking allows the creation and development of networks of online social relations— friendships and associations. Users can connect themselves with other users through consensual agreement. These connected users can communicate or exchange texts publicly and privately, as well as being able to share photos, music, movies, videos, and all other files of information that one wishes to share.

Millions access Facebook all the time searching for new friends or reconnecting old ones online and sharing information about important moments of their selves or with friends. Likewise, millions of viewers sign-in at YouTube to watch the latest audio and visual clippings, videos, movies, etc. every minute. For sharing their photos, Flickr happens to be the world's most favorite photo storage and sharing site, with Instagram not far behind.

Furthermore, if you are interested about knowing comprehensive definitions of a certain topic, word, phrase, or symbol, chances are that you will most likely check out the free online encyclopedia, or the Wikipedia site. For all you know, the history of Wikipedia tells and shows you the best description of the overwhelming power and rapid growth of social media.

The Wikipedia site enables anyone to contribute definitions, explanations, references, and various pertinent data and information of about anything under the sun. Nevertheless, anybody who may be interested to review the entries can do so.

In addition, they can comment, edit, remix, as well as provide further information or explanations to any of these entries. Therefore, what stirs up their interests is the collective effort of like-minded people who create, review and edit the topics.

Probably, this is the finest model of social media networking. As it is so, people congregate to communicate — hash out deliberations, discuss pros and cons of issues, and create contents that are informative and useful to everyone.

Upon <u>understanding the social media network from a marketing perspective</u>, you will be able to figure out a huge potential waiting for your business plans to explore further. Foremost, social media networks represent or correspond to a rich haven of online markets and attentive consumers.

With a readily available captive audience, your business can connect easily to its prospective consumers, who will be helping you to create an opinion or impression about your products or services. Additionally, your business can initiate with your prospects an interactive discussion regarding your products or services with the help of your concerned connections — previous and current consumers, as well as loyal customers.

By these vital interactions, you can receive real and sincere feedbacks about your brand from customers online. In short, you gain to learn invaluable insights from the shared experiences of consumers using your product or availing your service. Besides, you will have opportunities of fanning the flames of interest in others who are just watching on the sidelines and following the topic. Indeed, the phenomenon of social media marketing is a medium, which your business outfit must not ignore!

# The Basic Concept of Social Media Marketing

The dawn of social media began in 1978 when the original computer-based social network, Bulletin Board Systems (BBS) posted the first exchanged social data across phone lines with other users. The BBS, sometimes termed as computer bulletin board, was a computer server, which ran a program or application devoted to the disseminating, sharing, or exchanging of messages, data, or other files on a network.

Generally, the BBS referred to text-based online communities, where users were able to enter thru the Internet. However, when the Internet took off in full flight, consumers came to ignore and disregard totally these carefully drafted text messages. Instead, they took more control and authority over how they aired their respective experiences and sentiments with products and services.

From the message boards to websites, to blogs and online forums, conversations began springing up around businesses, brands, products, and companies. Most of these conversations possessed greater influences — on what others believe to be valuable, subscribe to, and buy — than any other messaging standard that the science of marketing could handle.

At present, social media marketing, and more specifically, social networks, are growing increasingly more important in terms of the purchasing decisions of consumers. For this reason, both fields have the capabilities of amplifying in vast proportions the basic aspect of advertising — word-of-mouth.

Fact is that social media marketing and social networks have even the strong potentials of becoming more significant, if not, greatly indispensable as opposed to traditional mainstream advertising being a trusted and reliable source of information. Nonetheless, it is noteworthy that in social media marketing, you have lesser control over positioning and messaging.

### *Definition of Social Media*

Social media pertains relatively to genuine and self-generated conversations transpiring between people concerning a certain topic of mutual interest, developed on the notions and experiences of the involved participants. Hence, social media is absolutely all about sharing or exchanging and aiming to drive towards a collective vision, which often intends to present more appropriately informed choices, options, and decisions at the end.

For its coverage, social media encompasses a wide assortment of online and mobile platforms of open discussion or word-of-mouth forums. It includes to name a few:

- Blogs or weblogs
- Company-sponsored chatrooms and discussion boards
- Consumer-to-consumer email
- Consumer product/service rating sites and forums,
- Internet forums and discussion boards
- Sites that stores and shares digital images, audio, or videos

💻 Social networking websites

Social networks — interchangeably termed as social media sites — are the primary components of the social media web. Typically, social networks refer to online communities and sub-groups of like-minded people who usually share a mutual interest or common activity. Inherent to these sites is having the ability to facilitate the communication process, which provides a variety of procedures for its users to interact.

The nature of social media continues to grow at all levels of society. According to a recent statistical study conducted by the global inbound marketing and sales developer, HubSpot, it showed that although 9 out of 10 internet users among the 18 to 24 age group use social media sites thru any device for at least once a month, social media extends persistently its influences to all the other age groups. Age groups above 35 years old, however, manifest much higher rates of social media users and usage.

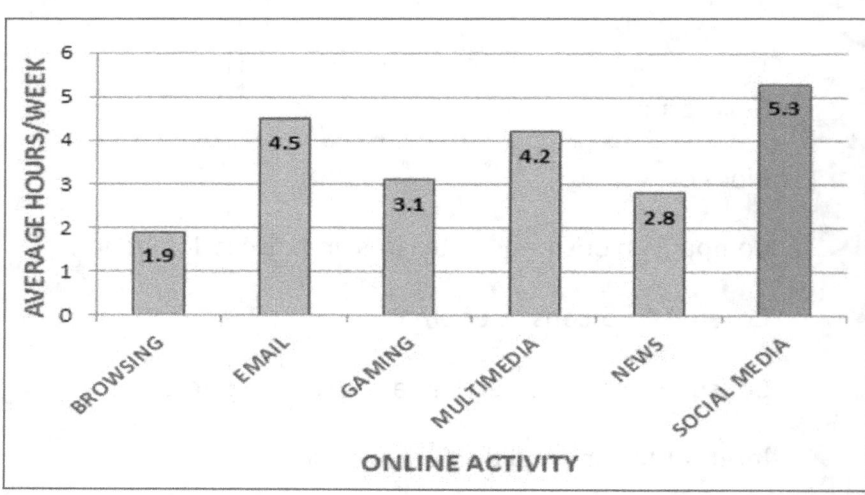

Image – 2: Charted Data of Average Hours per Week Spent on Online Activities Worldwide

Moreover, the study recorded the average hours spent per week by these age groups on online activities. It pointed to the fact that the entire world is becoming more and more social than it ever was, posting an average of 5.1 hours/week spent on social media (refer to Image-2).

In addition, social media evolves constantly and changes over time. On one hand, it allows users to generate contents and comments in real time and in an interactive or participative manner whenever they desire to add any further pieces of information.

Thus, by its nature of having quick-changing contents and comments, a stream of users builds up to a steady flow of traffic just to watch out for, and comment further to the latest updates, or simply follow the message threads.

On the other hand, it has been a given that social media subjects itself to undergo regularly modifications with replacement or additional features. It is integral to the supreme technologies of the Internet, as well as to the urgent calls of the changing times.

*Definition of Social Media Marketing*

Social media marketing applies social media sites to increase levels of visibility on the Web and to promote brands, products, and services of the business. However, to echo this chapter's **opening quote,** social media marketing is actually a unique type of commercial promotion that trains exclusively its focus on people… not on products/services… much less, not on your business!

The following are basic examples of social media marketing techniques that make excessive use of social media sites to the advantage of your business:

💻 Join relevant social networking sites or dynamic online communities that can certainly help promote your business, brand, product or service.

💻 Install the RSS web feeds to your website so that users can access or re-purpose easily the updates to online content, as well as allowing them to keep track of your various websites in just a single news aggregator.

💻 Create your business weblog (or a website consisting of your series of blog entries, which you update frequently with new information about specific topics about your business).

💻 Use the optimal functionalities of the following promotional tools: blogs, folksonomies, message boards, news sharing, online videos, podcasts (audio and video files), photo sharing, social curation, social networking site postings, and wikis, to establish a larger fan base and reach a wider targeted audience.

As a staunch marketer, you may present your products or services with as many promotional tools and qualitative features as possible; yet, what truly matters most, in the end, are those positive comments and words of appreciation, as well as constructive criticisms that your customers leave.

However, the common reason why most marketers perceive social media marketing to be challenging and scary is the fact that it is a constituent of the second generation of the World Wide Web or the Web 2.0 trend.

Web 2.0 refers to the collective term of innovative modifications in the design and usage of websites and web pages. Essentially, it emphasizes the ability of end-users to generate content, collaborate and share pertinent data and information online, and interoperate dynamically within the virtual world of the Internet.

**Henceforth,** being a function and part of the Web 2.0, social media marketing supports the Web 2.0 principle of *'user empowerment.'* Fundamentally, this indicates that the people are the ones generating the content. You are no longer in full control of your brand's marketing content unlike in traditional advertising.

This also implies that negative contents or comments can occur inevitably. Consequently, these damaging messages will certainly spread like wildfire the world over in just a matter of a few seconds!

As social media transmits these Internet-based contents and messages with a vigorous ripple effect, they become now the principal factor in influencing several aspects of the consumers' emotional, mental, and behavioral responses (i.e., awareness, attitudes, consideration, collation of information, impressions, opinions, perceptions, purchasing decisions, post-purchase assessment, etc.).

Therefore, as a global marketer, you need to recognize the critical nature and potential force of the conversations made by the empowered consumers using social media. In effect, the chief quality required from you or your marketing team is developing and nurturing the ability to influence effectively the empowered crowd.

## Importance of Social Media Marketing in Your Business

**As a process of promoting your brand or business thru the various channels and platforms of social media networks, social media marketing becomes a powerful promotional strategy that will deliver the following:**

💻 Attention or awareness of your products or services;

💻 Huge volumes of steady traffic to your business outfit, website or weblog; and,

💻 Enormous opportunities for hitting increased sales revenues.

To the most evident or extreme degree, no other <u>cost-effective marketing methodology</u> will easily provide you ready access to the exponential numbers of prospective consumers for your business. **To those ignoring social media, they usually fall into these following categories:**

💻 Those who never knew anything much about social media

💻 Those who had the interest but just never knew how to use it

💻 Those who never believed in the value of how a social media marketing strategy can bring home success to a business

Moreover, with the availability of social media metrics and analytics, social media marketing enables you to listen, track, and evaluate the messages shared on social media sites. Thus, this gives you the opportunity of improving and adapting to the needs of your customers. After all, people never expect your business to be perfect; rather, they always expect it to provide solutions!

With the growing throngs of people worldwide aboard the bandwagon of joining social media networks and using them in a regular and efficient manner, the rosy industry of social media is here to stay and foresees itself growing much bigger in the upcoming years. The following are some interesting statistics that are undoubtedly telltale signs for your business to leverage its application of social media in order to keep pace with the competition and survive amidst the rapidly changing moments:

💻 Adult users of social media have risen sharply from a measly 7% in 2005 to 85% just within a dozen of years later.

💻 Usage of social media through mobile and other handheld devices has registered a steady annual growth of 30%.

💻 More than two million business entities in the world at present continuously use social media sites advertising for promoting their brands, products, and services.

For such amazing figures and growths, businesses today — including yours, of course — ought to take advantage of the overflowing graces of social media and to leverage the business with the proper social media platforms in the best way possible. Do it not because social media is the current craze or everything about it seems sounding simple; but rather, indulge in it because your target market is hanging around at all the popular social media networks! For all you know, they are NOW engaging with all their favorite brands, products, and services!

> "Social media is here. It is not going away and not a passing fad. Be where your customers are: in social media."
>
> — **Lori Ruff**

# Chapter 3 – Effects of SMM on Consumers' Purchasing Responses: The Social Feedback Cycle

*"Social media allows big companies to act small again."*

— **Jay Baer**

It has long been a potential consumer's habit to consider certain prerequisites prior to making any purchases, whether urgent or not. The most common among these necessary pre-purchasing factors are making comparisons with the counterpart brands of competitors and learning more information about each brand, product or service.

As they do so nowadays, consumers usually use and rely on the Internet or the search engines as their primary source of information about the brand. Alternatively, they interact with their family and friends thru social networking sites to collate opinions or recommendations. Furthermore, they search for the brand in other social media channels to read critical reviews and conversations about first-hand experiences and feedbacks— positive or negative — from people who had previously used the brand. Actually, social media marketing studies indicate that almost 70% of the conversations online refer to certain brands, products or services.

With this almost intrinsic consumer behavior, as well as their unrelenting dependency of sourcing information from the Web, it is truly prudent for any social media marketing endeavors to take into account the effects or influences of social media on the buying behaviors of consumers.

To facilitate your understanding on this regard would be a presentation of the comparative analyses of the *'traditional purchase funnel theory'* and the *'contemporary social feedback cycle.'*

**On one hand,** the purchase funnel theory is a consumer-focused marketing model, which describes the theoretical journey of a particular customer towards purchasing a certain product or service. The theory's funnel analogy implies the systematical narrowing down of the purchasing process by a fully aware customer by weighing options, making decisions, and ultimately purchasing the product **(refer to Image-3)**.

Based on the illustration of Image-3, you can quickly surmise the triumvirate stages of the traditional purchase funnel theory — awareness, consideration, and purchase. You can actually add more stages along the funnel depending upon the nature and substance of your strategic marketing plan, to name a few: familiarity, opinion, intent, advocacy, loyalty, and preference. Nonetheless, those cited and illustrated stages are just the most fundamental ones.

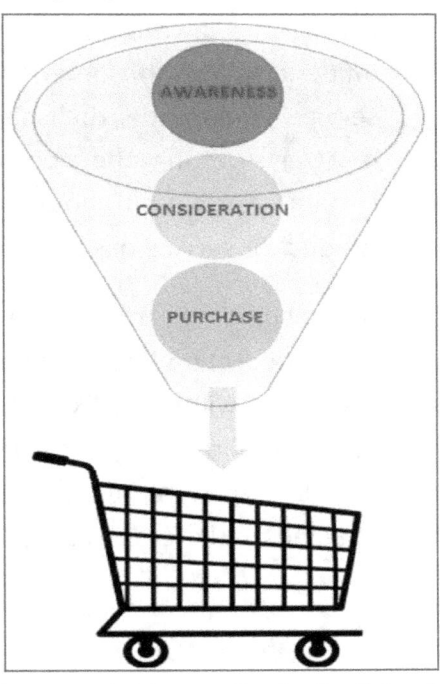

*Image – 3: Diagram for the Traditional Marketing Model of the Basic Purchase Funnel Theory*

In this marketing model, too many marketers have usually utilized less in their strategic marketing plan the halfway stage of consideration, where customers consider evaluating their purchase options. Instead, most of these marketers concentrated heavily and put a premium on the initial stage of awareness.

For this reason, the old school of thought taught that consumers' awareness of a brand spurs demand; and thereby, upon the point-of-sale, the factor of awareness would either affirm the other pending purchases or cause the potential customers shifting to a competing brand. Fact is that this has been the marketing practice for over the past fifty years or so.

During the awareness stage, marketers wield the power of influencing the consumers' awareness of the brand, product, or service. Apparently, their aim in their marketing plan's messages is always letting the consumer become completely aware of certain information about the brand and the details of what the product or service has to offer.

As consumers become more aware of the product, the next stage of consideration becomes merely an assumptive process that the consumer will more likely choose the brand when making their eventual purchasing decision. Thus, by this traditional marketing template anchored upon an awareness-focused marketing plan, it enabled marketers to corner substantial market shares.

On the other hand, the new era version of the consumer purchase funnel theory fundamentally applies and integrates social media as a tool during the consideration phase (weighing of options), which connects directly to the consummated purchase stage along the purchasing process.

The social feedback cycle begins its loop at the post-purchase experiences shared by the previous customer around social networking sites. This social feedback loop connects subsequently with the thought-processes of the next potential customers who progress eventually from the initial phase of awareness towards the purchasing stage **(refer to Image-4)**.

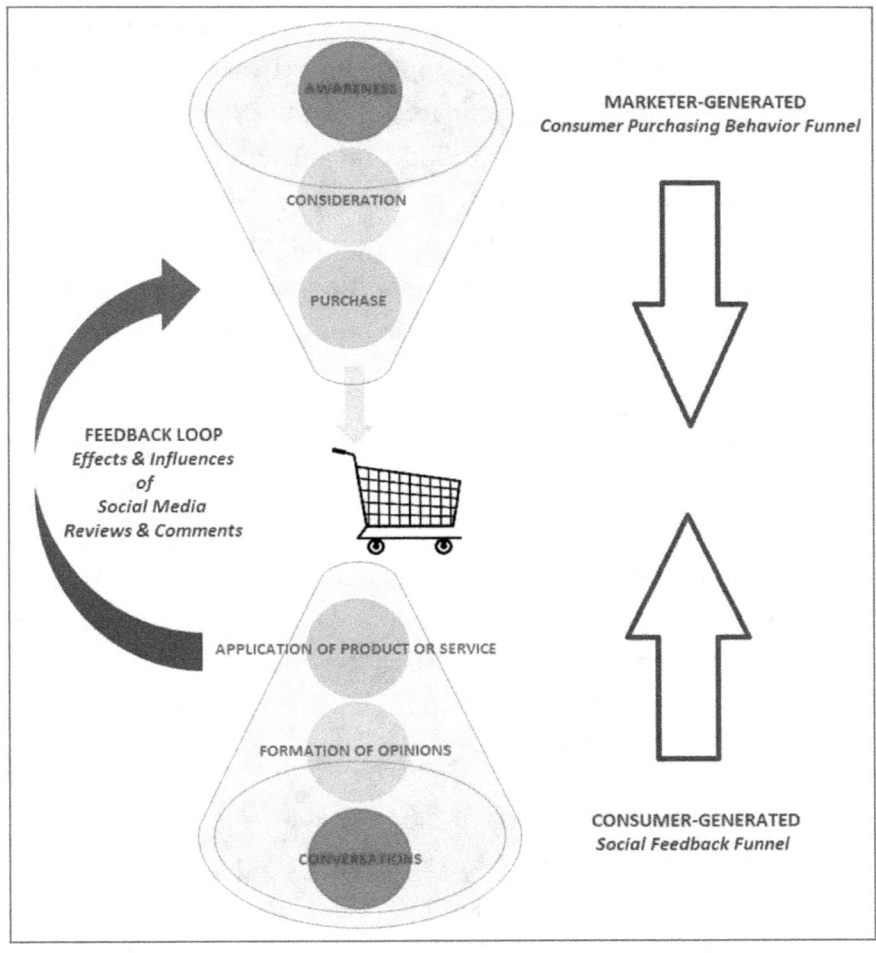

*Image – 4: Diagram for the New Era Marketing Model with the Social Feedback Cycle Theory*

The social feedback loop essentially describes the relationship of interdependence of the pre-and post-purchasing stages over time. In other words, in relation to the purchase funnel theory, what takes place at present (post-purchasing) will certainly affect what materializes in the future (pre-purchasing stage). As the cycle goes on over time, you achieve a definite pattern of a development.

**The feedback loop, created through using social media, bears the social media awareness, opinions, reviews, and comments transpiring from the conversed and shared experiences of respective customers who had previously purchased or used the brand.** From the consumer-generated social feedback funnel, the loop weaves its way back into the marketer-generated purchase funnel at the stage of consideration and becomes an integral element of the following cycle and the subsequent purchase evaluation process.

In substance, these opinions of the feedback loop weigh far more with value and considered more reliable and credible than any information or marketing message provided by marketers. **In fact, according to a recent consumer survey from Ambassador Advertising Agency,** 78% of consumers worldwide adjudge that they trust other customers' opinions and recommendations for brands, products, and services from social media more than any other available medium.

Indeed, the classic word-of-mouth advertising remains the basic, and yet, the most trustworthy source of information in the new era of social media marketing. Therefore, social media directly influences the purchase decisions and behaviors of the consumers since they usually seek nowadays the opinions, comments, reviews, and recommendations of others in social media.

To support further the conclusive statement about social media's strong impact on consumers, the survey from Ambassador also stated that 71% of global customers have a high likelihood of recommending or referring a particular brand to others on social media, especially when they have a great and positive experience with the brand. This is chiefly because consumers see other consumers as more objective than the companies' own marketing message. Consumers are undistorted by emotion or personal bias.

In details, once customers have consummated purchasing a brand, product, or service, they will be using it, experiencing its upsides and downsides, and forming their personal opinion of it. Apparently, they will then relate their respective personal experiences with the brand, product, or service through the Internet, more particularly, by accessing the various social media platforms.

These customers would have options of leaving a comment on the brand's official website or the different social media sites of the company. Additionally, they might join in general online forums where the marketers of the company might never see.

The conversation made and held by these customers on the social media platforms are open, or seen and read publicly, for other people or prospective customers who already have an awareness — either insufficient or substantial — about the brand, product, or service. Hence, these readers are actually in the consideration stage of the purchase funnel. They will search for further information about the brand, product, or service on the Internet, where they will find easily and quickly the contents in the form of comments, reviews, and opinions generated by those customers who have purchased and experienced the brand.

Since these consumer-generated conversations are typically objective sources of information, the prospective customers will certainly trust completely whatever appreciations or depreciations uttered by the previous customers. More often than not, these conversations become the primary bases of the purchase decisions of the prospective customers.

It turns out then that the consideration stage is the central link between marketing and the social web. Fundamentally, this is the core operations and connection of marketing based on social media.

Whereas then, the consideration stage of the purchase funnel has usually been an inaccessible grey area for marketers, it has now been extremely influenced by the consumer-generated contents shared on the various social media channels. This is also the reason why social customer service, or listening and responding to consumers in social media, is becoming more importantly necessary than ever before.

In conclusion, the social feedback cycle, which you have to develop and maintain over time, is one of the most powerful marketing planning tools that you need to take into account as a social media marketing professional, especially when developing your social media marketing strategies.

Therefore, to be a successful social media marketer, your best challenging option will then be spending more of your time on how to use effectively social media, apply the social feedback cycle, and getting the marketing and operations relationship of your business right.

## Importance of Social Customer Service

In terms of managing the relationships of your business with your customers, it is a mortal sin to neglect or disregard totally the great opportunity of customer service through social media. Since there is a continuing rise in the number of customers who expect to receive or avail *'social customer service,'* this becomes necessarily urgent for brands and business to listen emphatically, as well as to respond as quickly as possible to the voices of the customers — either appreciative or depreciative.

More than ever, consumers generally turn to the Internet or social media to find solutions when they experience problems with a brand. Based again on the recent consumer survey from Ambassador Advertising Agency, more than 50% of all social media users engage with brands several times a month, with about 10% of them are engaging with brands on a daily basis.

Is your business completely prepared to face all these issues? Social media studies and their data **(refer to Image-5)** suggest that the ability of your business to manage customer service via the different social media outlets can turn complaints into future sales revenues. By leveraging social engagement, you and your business can build brand loyalty and turn users into fans and advocates.

If your business is still wavering and contending whether or not it has the urgent need to relate and engage with customers through social media platforms, then ponder on the fact why 73% of all the top-performing companies in the world have engaged in social media. Their main reason was... customer service!

# SOCIAL Consumer Service
RELATIONS TO SOCIAL MEDIA MARKETING & BUILDING LOYAL CUSTOMERS

**71%** of online customers expect to receive assistance within 5 minutes after they reach out to a company

If they do not receive any form of assistance, **48%** will leave the site.

If they receive great customer service via social media, they are more likely to spend **21% MORE.**

**RECOMMENDED!**

**19%** of customers who do not receive a response will still recommend the company.

**RECOMMENDED!**

**71%** of customers who have a positive customer service experience via social media are likely to recommend the company.

Image – 5: Infographic of a Compilation of 2017 Social Media Studies on Social Customer Service

According to the facts of the infographic, social customer service truly implies to be a compelling opportunity for your business. It demonstrates the advantages of having quick response times (QRTs), as well as the positive effects of QRTs on the consumer's brand engagements.

The challenge, therefore, will be how your business or brand can create and render a satisfactory social customer service experience, which will keep consumers from coming back and knocking at your door for more. Aside from responding to your customers as swiftly as possible, showing them some personality is one of the most basic and significant factors you must require on your social consumer service programs. Discover more salient factors as you will read along.

## Learning Approach for Marketing Professionals about the Social Web

If the Web has affected the lives of billions of people across the globe and led them congregating together through social media outlets, the same tools and technology have reinvented the media and marketing campaign strategies for the marketing outfits too. No major business today can ever ignore the social web!

In fact, all types of businesses have used social media effectively, from home store depots for their extensive product lines and product catalogs to Hollywood films for their premier releases. In addition, these businesses have harnessed efficiently and exploited the power of social media sites for generating an instant awareness about their brand, product, or service.

Owing to the fact that the presence and participation of consumers in the social web are mostly about the engagement with a product or service, the marketing outfit of your business must also be present so you can address your prospective buyers who are listening to the feedback from those who have already bought and used your product or service.

As mentioned previously, **marketing practitioners or professionals like you ought to integrate the application of social media into your respective marketing campaigns. You should also incorporate this integration with all the rest of your media channels upon which you are currently using.**

The kickoff point of your learning approach about the social web shall be to understand comprehensively the technology, how the social web functions, the diverse world of social media channels, as well as the programs of each platform.

Your understanding of the common behaviors of these participants all over the social web channels is very significant since this audience is what your marketing outfit is actually all concerned about in the first place. This congregation of people consists of your current customers and prospects or would-be customers of your company. Hence, you should be realizing by now the huge potentials existing in the ability to reach out to a larger and broader consumer base at a minuscule cost.

The next phase of the learning curve is to observe and understand what eventualities occur on the social web whenever individuals or communities are conversing to one another across the social networks.

The aspect of consumer awareness can result in either positive or negative publicity. Hence, you should be able to influence, if not, control directly the reactions of the audience through well-orchestrated and smoothly designed participation in the discussions and events on the social web.

Another aspect that is more prominent and distinctive among the users of social media is the trust factor. Generally, participants involved in the discussions trust without a doubt each other's words. Thus, even if a business participates in the discourse, and thereby, influences the discussion, then everyone assumes that all the communicated words are 100% true.

**It becomes crucial on the part of the business, therefore, to ensure the content of the discussion must be the truth and it should deliver its promises. You must always keep in mind that the current customers would only start judging the product or service depending upon the satisfaction levels and extent of benefits they obtained from the product or service vis-à-vis their expectations of it.**

Hence, as a marketing professional, it would be important for you understand also how the discussions and conversations in social media will function to be an effective or positive feedback to the prospective consumers. Any feedback is responsible for building the awareness of the consumers, and more importantly, for influencing their behavior and decision to ultimately purchase. **Furthermore,** it is a necessity for you to synchronize all your business operations with your social media campaign across the social media outlets, in such a way as to deliver whatever commitments or promises your business offered.

# E-Commerce Inbound Marketing

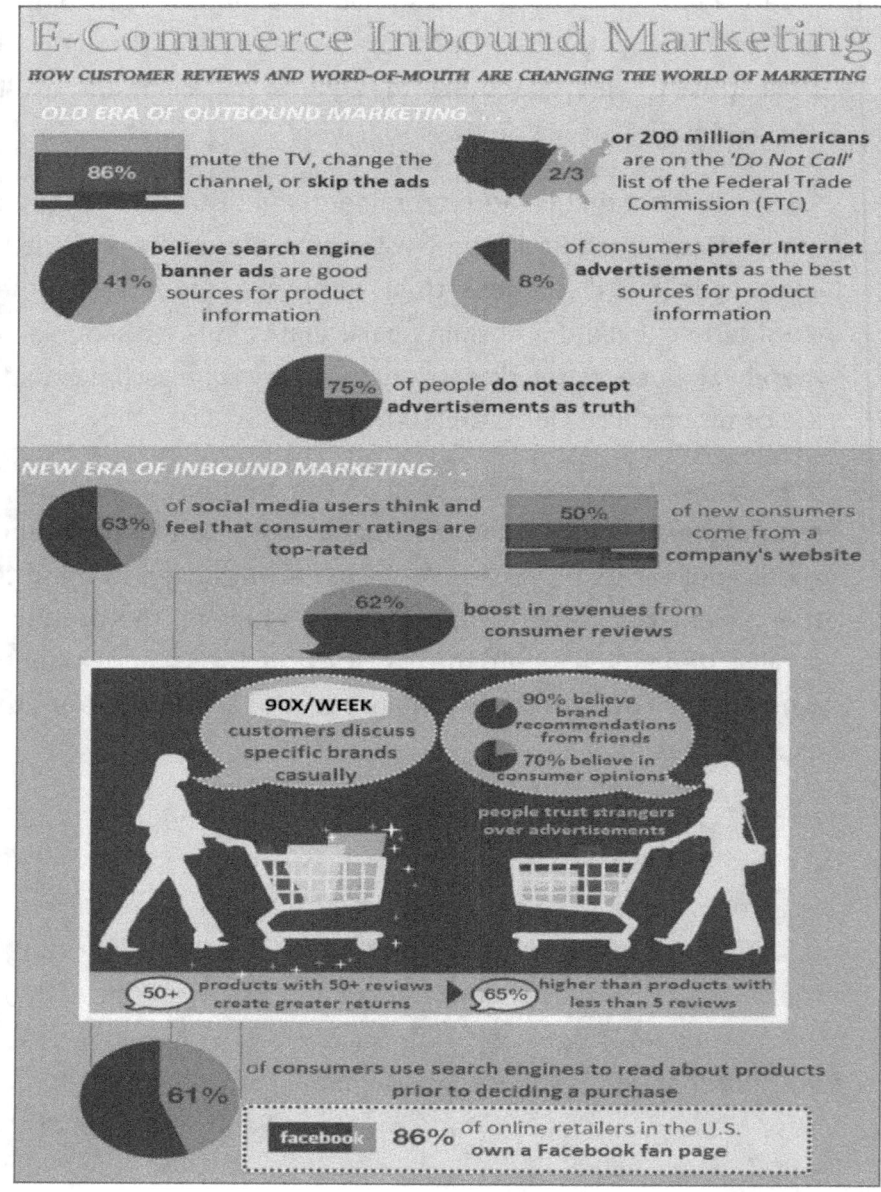

Image – 6: Infographic of the New Era of E-Commerce Inbound Marketing

The preceding image is a visual presentation of the various and helpful information on e-commerce inbound marketing that will guide you towards <u>creating the essential elements of your ideal and systematic social media marketing strategy</u>:

In the realm of social media marketing, everyone is talking about *'e-commerce inbound marketing'*. As a primer, e-commerce inbound marketing is a technical marketing process for attracting the attention of both customers and prospects to brands, products, and services via social media marketing, content creation or digital content marketing, search engine optimization, social media optimization, and branding. In short, e-commerce inbound marketing is one of the ideal and cost-effective marketing methods for lead conversion, developing a business website, and growing a successful business.

Consumers nowadays connect each other, rate products and services, and discuss and digest product reviews and information like never before. Actually, they comprise the powerful and influential online presence for all types, levels, and scales of e-commerce businesses.

Under this emerging social revolution, an investment in e-commerce inbound marketing makes it capable and possible for businesses that are into e-commerce or e-business (commerce conducted electronically, as on the Internet) to take advantage of;

💻 Increased opportunities for driving social media traffic and growing online sales

💻 Reduce the cost of customer acquisition (COCA)

💻 Strengthens the retention of new customers

This should no longer come as a surprise since its customer-focused approach to marketing help continuously a brand to get the buzz of a dynamic online marketplace to reach effectively its target customers. Although several e-commerce businesses rely typically on digital advertising to highlight their products, available and possible opportunities are aplenty for e-commerce brands that would like to take an integrated consumer engagement plan of reaching their target market and receiving authoritative reviews about their products or services by way of inbound methods. To understand better how it works, inspect the basic e-commerce inbound marketing methodology map (refer to Image-7):

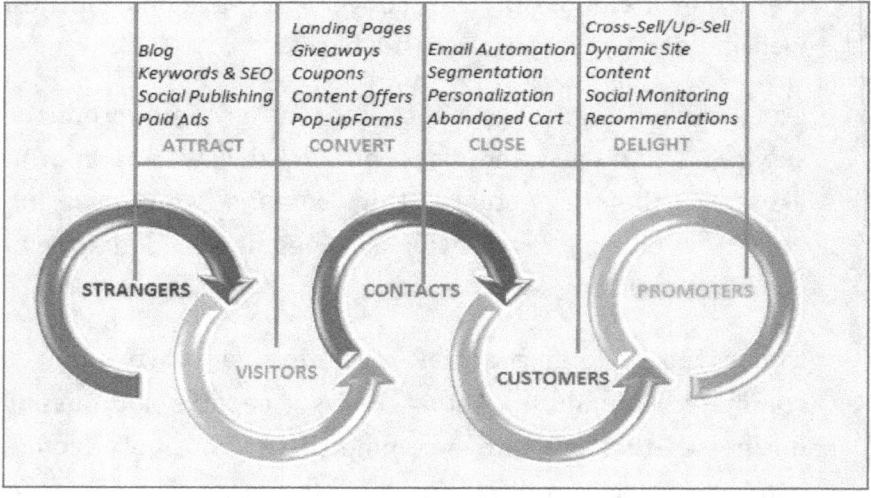

*Image – 7: Methodology of E-Commerce Inbound Marketing*

**The principal reason why does e-commerce inbound marketing work for business is that its methodology is entirely about driving your target customers to your end through quality contents (which include positive product reviews) and other significant areas of interaction.**

Instead of showing paid ads to your target consumers and waiting impatiently for them to click, you build a library of interesting, valuable, and informative contents that will help your business build trust and goodwill, which stimulate interest and conversion within your target audience.

*"Word-of-mouth marketing is not about giving customers talking points as if they were brand spokespeople. It is about delivering an exceptional customer experience that makes customers want to recommend you."*

— **Deborah Eastman**

# Chapter 4 – Purposes and Benefits of Social Media Marketing

*"Social media will help you build up the loyalty of your current customers to the point that they will willingly, and for free, tell others about you."*

— **Bonnie Sainsbury**

Several top businesses in this new era of advertising subscribe to social media marketing since it corresponds to cost-effective marketing solutions. Foremost, the tools used widely in social media marketing are free, not to mention about their user-friendliness, as opposed to other promotional tools.

Furthermore, the following are the other central purposes and benefits of integrating social media marketing in their business strategies, with each item devoted to an in-depth discussion in entirely separate sections:

💻 Brand Awareness or Product/Service Exposure

💻 Demographic and Geographic Targeted Traffic

💻 Lead Generation and Conversion

💻 Market Research Insights and Competitor Analyses

💻 Social Customer Service, Consumer Interaction, and Feedbacks

💻 Cost-Effective Marketing Solutions

💻 Public Relations and Social Recruitment System of Human Resources

Actually, the purposes and benefits of social media marketing can be boundless as it grows with time. The aforementioned sections only comprise a synopsis about its general marketing purposes, which cover:

- Generation of new marketing strategy concepts
- Online reputation and communications management
- Search engine optimization and website traffic
- Co-innovation with consumers or business partnerships
- Customer loyalty development
- Development of new brands, products, or services
- Amplification of the marketing pitch thru word-of-mouth

***The fundamentals of social media marketing are essentially the applications of powerful unconventional means to attain successful conventional ends. Generally, these guerrilla marketing methods and non-conformist strategies are the implementations of social media creativity, user empowerment or community participation, and goodwill relationships rather than the traditional huge advertising budgets to realize the various marketing objectives.***

At present, every marketer like you is equipped fully with highly effective and efficient online communication tools, which enable you to acquire similar extents of influence that several big corporations have exclusively possessed before. The marketing arena is now already a level playing field, and social media marketing is the great game changer in the kingdom of marketing.

Prior to learning the purposes and benefits of social media marketing, it would also be noteworthy to study some important statistics of the efforts and commitments of social media users, as compiled from various credible global marketing agency sources (HubSpot, WordStream, SocialMediaExaminer, Ambassador, etc.). The common denominator manifests theoretical analyses, which imply to the apparent existence of the vast gains, assistance, usefulness, and potentials that social media marketing offers.

💻 9 out of 10 or 94% of social media marketers worldwide affirmed that they apply social media for marketing objectives

💻 83% of these global social media marketers confirmed that social media offers several significant benefits for the growth and success of the business, whether it may concern small and medium-scale enterprises or those large corporations and multinationals

💻 8 out of 10 or 81% of all registered small and medium-sized businesses use social media platforms that are more social or with a broader mass population base

💻 9 out of 10 or 91% of global retail brands use a couple or more social media networks

💻 The world's population of active social media users stands at 3.03 billion, growing at a rate of one new social media user for every quarter of an hour (as recorded with the additional growth of 121 million new users during the last quarter of 2017)

💻 About 60% of the world's marketers use social media for more than 6 hours weekly; and, 33% for more than 11 hours during the same frequency

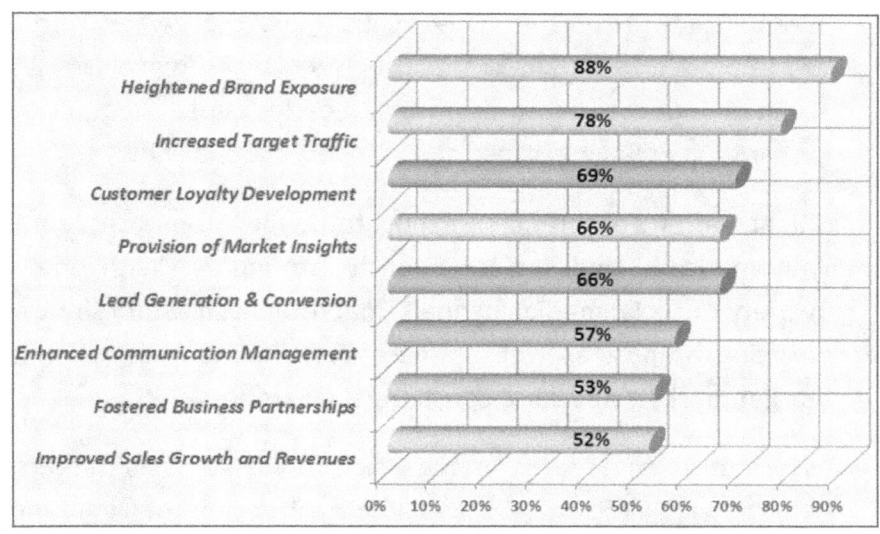

*Image – 8: Purposes and Benefits of Social Media Marketing Survey Results from Social Media Marketers*

## Brand Awareness or Product/Service Exposure

Social media sites promote clear communication and fresh information circulated widely around brands, products, and services. However, these exchanges or transmission of informative messages either enhances positive or emphasizes negative word-of-mouth.

Thousands, if not, millions of people can see and read any messages or pieces of information shared on the social web just within an extremely short period, actually, in seconds. Hence, people become aware quickly and easily; and truly, it is a no-brainer why a heightened brand awareness or product/service exposure is the principal benefit received by businesses applying social media strategies (refer to Image-8).

Brand exposure ensues when consumers are being aware of a certain advertisement, product, or service through exercising, at least, one of their faculties of sight, hearing, smell, taste, or touch, regardless of paying attention to the exposure or not.

Right after a brand's exposure, word-of-mouth amplifies automatically and instantaneously around it. With the wide variety of social media channels, marketers can establish new and existing brands, as well as increasing their brands' visibility to target markets and raise consumers' awareness.

Consumers' awareness of the brand presents to marketers and businesses alike several possibilities of building the reputation of their brand and increase its popularity. Specifically, this marketing procedure is termed as *'online reputation management.'*

Therefore, the primary step to brand exposure, especially for new brands, is to set up your pages and improve on your profiles on social media platforms where your brand becomes visible and reaches its target audience. **Sans any exposures, your brand will certainly fail upon its launching.**

Furthermore, you can use social media platforms to promote your products and services. **The social media pages of your brand will provide you great opportunities for presenting your products and services in a manner that is more interactive.**

For the part of the consumers, however, they will have options of either reading the description of your product or seeing its pictures or watch the videos. Alternatively, they will be either reading comments or reviews about it, or simply ignoring them all. Hence, this implies enhancing your inbound marketing tactics.

Through social media marketing, it can increase consumers' awareness of your brand by extending (the duration for its visibility/exposure) and expanding (the reach of <u>demographic and geographic target markets</u>) with its online presence. This means that it would be extremely important for you to measure the effects of social media marketing on your brand awareness programs through using social media metrics.

**According to social media marketing specialists,** you should be taking into account three major social media metrics in the context of the lead generation or sales funnel, when evaluating measurements for brand awareness. These metrics are social media engagement, influence, and exposure. **The lead generation or sales funnel (refer to Image-9) shows the traditional flow of the ROI from the created programs of brand awareness.**

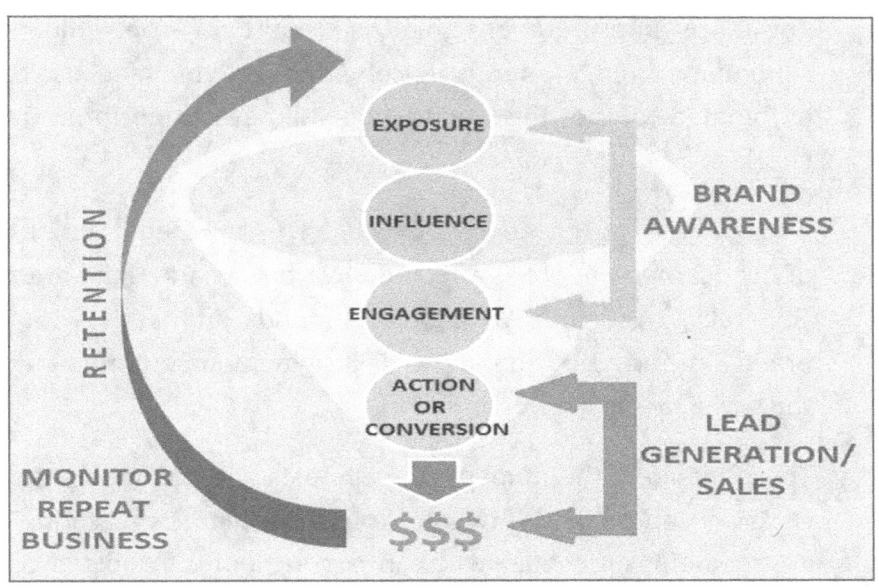

*Image – 9: Diagram of the Lead Generation or Sales Funnel with the Social Media Metrics for Evaluating Brand Awareness*

🖥 <u>Social Media Exposure Evaluation</u> – denotes the number of people for whom the marketing message reaches or the extent of the targeted market attracted to your brand via social media. This includes the number of citations of your brand, views, visits subscribers, fans, and followers.

However, tracking these metrics might necessitate complex efforts since it oftentimes requires you to perform manually the monitoring process. Besides, you might encounter difficulties avoiding duplication and separating the unique users.

🖥 <u>Social Media Influence Evaluation</u> – actually figures out the effects of the engagement evaluation results. These effects are more subjective or perceptual matters and depend on the business' perspectives of positive, negative, or neutral impacts.

They are interpretations of the report of top influencers, sentiments, and a shared voice. Although you may use some automated tools in this regard, you still have to perform manual checking.

🖥 <u>Social Media Engagement Evaluation</u> – represents the number of concerned people affected by the marketing message. Generally, this group of people responds intimately with your brand's message by sharing their insights and sentiments across the social media networks.

These manifest the number of wall posts and comments, shares, clicks, @ replies, and retweets. You can facilitate measuring such engagement processes with an assortment of tools available online.

Brand awareness, or interchangeably, brand exposure, is the primary phase of your relationship with consumers. **During this initial stage, the customer comes in without knowing or hearing anything about your brand at its first launching or exposure.**

Getting people exposed to your brand for their very first time, perhaps, upon reading some posts anywhere on the social media networks, will enable them to know that your brand is active and making waves online. Brand exposure in social media provides them with a more convenient and nonconfrontational way of taking them a step closer to, and on a more personal level with your brand, product, or service.

Therefore, an absolute must for your social media marketing strategy is to create a social media-optimized presence to heighten the online awareness of your brand. **For, after all, social media signals have now been starting to become key players in the organic search rankings.**

With social media optimization initiatives, your business can receive powerful boosts in your search engine optimization efforts. **As it is now apparently important ensuring your brand to receive the appropriate exposures in social media networks,** you should be able to establish and develop a powerful voice of your brand.

Consequently, amplify the general feel of your brand with the assistance of high quality and informative contents, inbound marketing, an enticing social media profile design, and a brand tone that reflects your business vision and mission statement. In the end, all these will contribute greatly towards providing your current and potential customers an enhanced experience.

## Demographic and Geographic Targeted Traffic

Directing a marketing message or targeted campaign becomes a breeze with the assistance and application of social media channels. Primarily, social media supports the basic concept of social media marketing of driving your product or service to a targeted audience, which always has the strong probability of being convinced to buy in.

In turn, social media networks will be driving targeted visitors back to your business website. The more social media channels you are using, then the more you will be receiving interested referrals, as well as backlinks pointing back to your website.

With their billions of member-users, social media networks truly provide businesses the ideal and convenient avenue for reaching huge target market bases that can even be unlimited in scope. Besides, social media marketing is a very effective means to draw in targeted traffic to your business website or weblog.

Before anything else, it would be important to define the basic term, *'traffic,'* prior to defining the more compound term, *'targeted traffic.'* Traffic exists whenever a user visits your website.

There are several techniques for receiving website traffic, and these tactics can easily provide your website thousands of visitors daily. Nevertheless, if you were not able to target specifically your traffic, then your throng of visitors would not probably care much or become interested with your brand, much less, in purchasing your product or service.

**In other words,** it is a targeted traffic whenever visitors reach a particular site and develop keen interests in purchasing your offered product or service after they have read an ad of your product or service that you promoted on that website. Being deeply concerned and interested to know more information about your brand, they consequently click on your ad link, which leads them to visit your business website.

Targeting specifically customers based on certain demographic and geographic parameters are among the most desirable abilities offered to marketers by advertising or marketing through social media. The software applications, which are at the easy disposal of various social media networks, are very helpful for demographic and geographic traffic targeting. A paid Facebook advertisement is the finest representation for such targeting.

*Generally, social media sites store their member-users' various personal information such as interests, geographical location, and demographical data like gender, race, age, religion, and occupation. Their reliable software applications have the ability to pre-select the respective profiles and locations of their users for which marketers can readily use all these data to reach their target audience.*

Hence, marketers are easily able to deliver directly their marketing messages to the consumers who have the most likelihood of noticing and clicking on them. Gone were the days when you lost your message to a particular segment of the market base that was never interested or concerned in the first place. Indeed, this social media marketing ability creates an amazing world of difference throughout all niches.

If you are planning to run your marketing operations, you will already have prior knowledge as to the description and parameters of your target market. Now, what social media is enabling you to do is creating campaigns that will feed directly to your specific demographic and geographic target markets instantaneously.

Although social media optimization and social media per se have opened new windows of opportunities like generating excessively huge amounts of online traffic, search engine optimization would still play its key role in availing your regular website traffic. Besides, most of the top search engines (Google, Yahoo!, and Bing) will always have a soft spot for social media.

Search engines pay much attention to social media networks since these are interactive platforms aligning to their objectives of enhancing the user experience and providing real-time data. When your social media profile or web page or weblog garners the top spot on the search engine result pages (SERPs), these leading search engines will be boosting further the visitor traffic to your respective sites online.

In addition, social media has the ability to generate high-value incoming links back to your websites. This is simply because search engines trust social media outlets, which oftentimes tend to receive fast listings.

For instance, blogs remain to be significantly effective instruments for boosting regular website traffic. Based on a report from Hubspot, businesses that have regular blog entries (weekly, at the least) are able to gain 55% more website visitors monthly compared to those companies that never blog (refer to Image-10).

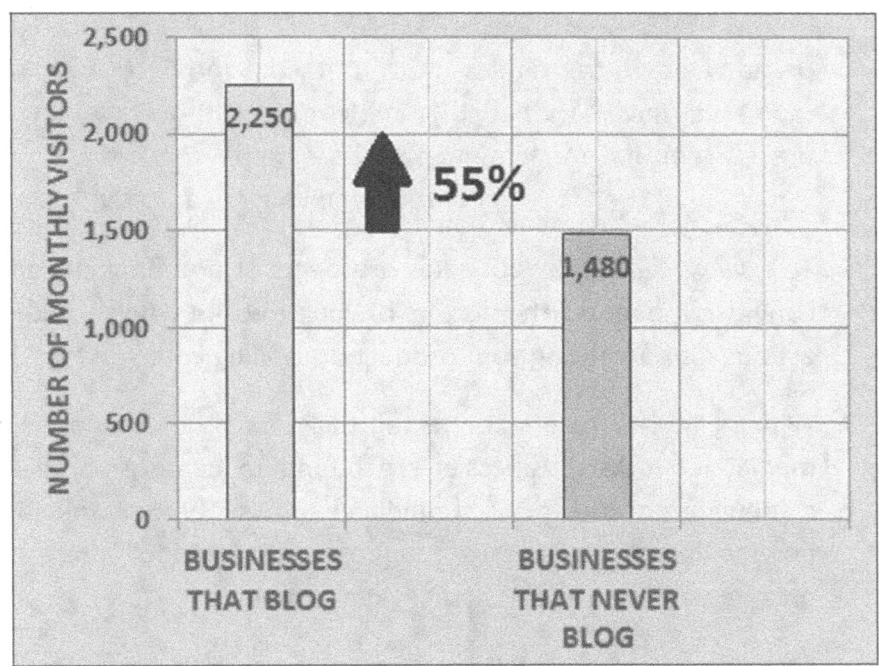

*Image – 10: Influence of Blogs on the Monthly Website Visitor Traffic for Businesses*

Social media is essentially all about building goodwill and trustworthy relationships. Therefore, the traffic generated entirely from social media networks can improve the perception of consumers about a brand.

Consumers trust businesses more when people they know are referring these companies. Consequentially, your business can receive regular traffic directly from your published quality contents on your social media pages, as well as from the audience who have read your content, commented or talked about it, liked it, and shared it online.

## Lead Generation and Conversion

Based again on the same report from HubSpot, 61% of American marketers have affirmed that their main purpose on why their organization has implemented a social media marketing strategy is to step-up their lead generation and conversion activities.

To review, leads are your sales prospects or potential customers; conversion denotes the visitors of your website who take desired actions, as purchasing your product or availing your service.

With millions of users connected daily across the various social media networks, businesses are bound to capture some leads somewhere on these social media channels. The only question is how will these businesses supposed to look for these sales prospects. The answer is actually quite simple.

Each individual who follows the Twitter profile of a particular business, or likes its Facebook page, is a potential customer. Hence, as businesses gain more and more fans and followers online, their brands can improve their chances of bringing forth new customers.

The utmost challenge for you here is encouraging people to pay a visit to the social media sites of your business. Nevertheless, not only their visiting acts are urgently necessary but more importantly, their reasons for spending more time on your site. **As soon as these visitors reach your site,** you must have to create and provide them enough value that may spur their interest or stir up their curiosities, opinions, feelings, and passions, for them to retain hanging around on your site.

To make your visitors spend more time on your social media sites, you should present your business efficiently and on more accommodating terms, and of course, dispose an air of politeness and friendliness. Initiate some connections with your visitors by allowing them to share valuable contents, providing helpful information, responding to any requests and critiques or positive or negative appraisals.

**Moreover,** you should create a unique persona to your brand and highlight it expressively on your social media sites. After your visitors become interested in your brand, only then will they become valuable leads.

**As always,** blogs play an extremely significant role to generate your leads. Take up the habit of posting blog entries that offer valuable information to your visitors to promote their interest in your brand's product or services.

According to the surveys from HubSpot, business-to-consumer (B2C) companies — business affairs or transactions managed or controlled directly between a business outfit and consumers, or the end-users of products or services — that are blogging regularly generate about 90% more leads monthly than others that do not.

Similarly, business-to-business (B2B) companies — referring to the trade and commerce conducted between two or more businesses, typically occurring when a company sources out its materials from another company — generate close to 70% more. Thus, either way, there is no doubt for your business benefitting from lead generation and conversion by implementing an interactive social media marketing strategy.

## Market Research Insights and Competitor Analyses

Social media and the World Wide Web have transformed completely the ways of gaining business insights through market research and knowledge about the competition through competitor monitoring analyses. Since the social media networks are entirely public, you can access easily specific information about your target audience, as well as your business competitors.

In short, the social media networks offer you the opportunity of spying on the competition. Besides, several tools are available online to help you analyze what your competitors are doing. As a result, you can watch closely and monitor the current activities of your competitor, read their weblogs, website, and social media sites.

Moreover, you can even pick from them a few clever tricks or nuggets of wisdom, which you may apply for your own business operations. Thus, social media readily facilitates collating significant insights in the marketplace to benchmark your competencies.

Competitive benchmarking is vitally integral to any social media marketing strategy. Every brand has its own sets of goals and objectives, strategies, and implementation tactics.

Nevertheless, brands and their rival counterparts are generally striving and jockeying to reach the same target market while also engaging with the same consumer information database in social media. Yet, you must not interpret social media as an instrument that merely garners artificial sales revenues.

Instead, social media should merely mirror how your business enterprise operates from day to day. First, your business deserves the right to examine how your competitors perform dynamically on their social media sites on a daily basis:

💻 How many social media sites have they created? How many of these sites are they updating regularly? What are the most commonly updated sites?

💻 How are they actually posting, when do they usually post, and what is the frequency of their posting?

💻 How do the people, or the markets, react to their posts?

When you come to understand the activities of your competitors, it provides you with important insights about which marketing strategy models are successful and which are not. **Hence, it further helps you towards your making the proper decisions without the expense, efforts, and risks of trying them out first.**

**Aside from knowing your competitors' respective activities online,** try to find out how do consumers feel about your competitor's brand, products, or services as they compare them with the other competitors offering the same. **In this way,** it helps your business to strengthen and emphasize its features that consumers like most. At the same time, this will enable you to make corresponding modifications where you feel the deficiencies of your business when matched against the rest of the competition.

On the LinkedIn business networking site, for example, you will be able to see usual company data like the number of employees and followers, and products or services offered, including other brand competitors commonly viewed by people (refer to Image-11).

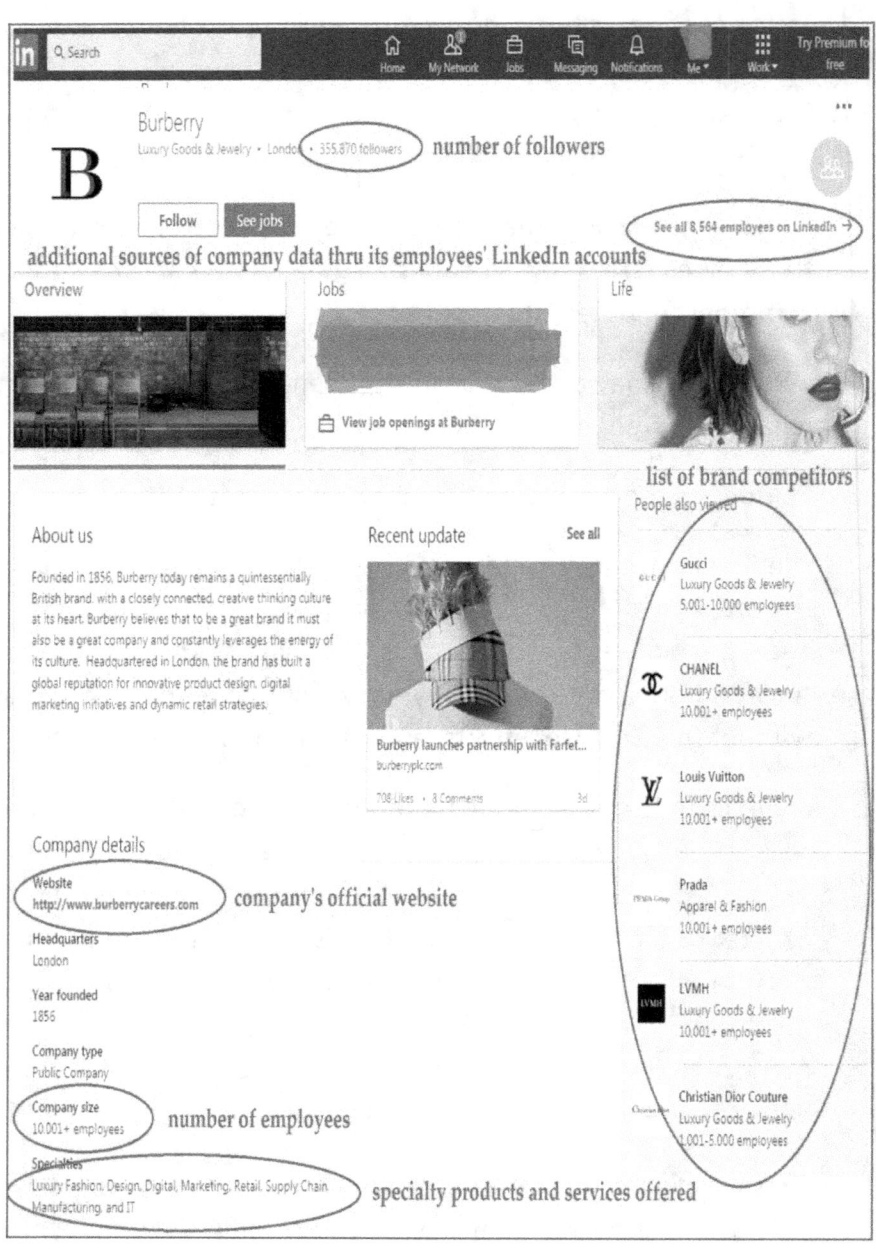

*Image – 11: Example of a Company's Social Media Profile (LinkedIn)*

Among the many free online tools that you can use, together with social media applications, to research for further valuable information about your competitors are:

💻 Hyper-Alerts – monitors new Facebook page comments

💻 Social Mention – a search engine for social media capable of searching user-generated content in real time like blogs, bookmarks, events, comments, news, and videos

💻 Twitter Advanced Search – follows ongoing conversations, specific tweets, and accounts by searching for topic hashtags or keywords

You can also set up Google Alerts so that you can receive messages each time the Internet uses specific keywords such as your competitors' brand names and the variations of their products or services. This free monitoring tool will further help you to track and see what consumers appreciate for, and complain against your competitors.

Monitoring techniques, with the help of these social media tracking tools, are great ways to discover which social media marketing strategies function better, and where your target market is. Alerts and notifications from these tools will provide you with insights into marketing techniques, programs, and strategies. They will also enable your brand to distinguish itself and remain in front of the pack of competitors.

Secondly, it is also worth for your business to see available data and information concerning directly the target audience on the social media networks. Analyzing these data would provide you extra information on the consumer demographics and behaviors.

Find out these individuals visiting your competitors' sites. Try to connect and follow with some; or, initiate interacting with others. Introduce them bit by bit to your brand and business until gradually enticing and converting them to close a sale.

Even though you may not have the ability to control what takes place in social media, you can always study what goes on and learn from it. Social media, therefore, can be comparable to a large and perpetually on-going *'focus group'* (a collective gathering of a demographically diverse group of individuals who continuously provide insights of consumer perceptions about brands and new products or services within an environment that is dynamically receptive, yet, non-threatening).

Both of your gathered information — from your competitors and target audience — will greatly influence and help to improve the social media marketing strategies of your business. It will further let you understand better your target audience and their expectations, needs, habit, and practices. More importantly, all these information enable you to use the ideal social media marketing techniques and design the adequate marketing message to reach directly your target market.

Lastly, social media networks offer you the opportunity of testing your designed marketing campaign strategies before finalizing your concrete social media marketing programs. These tests will help you to have a better grasp of what reaches your target market more effectively. In addition, the tests serve as cost-effective measures since you will be able to gather and collate feedbacks that influence decisions of accounting only the necessary marketing costs prior to spending more money on reaching out collectively to your target audience.

# Social Customer Service, Consumer Interaction, and Feedbacks

Social media networks also represent broad, valorized, and interactive communication between businesses and their current customers and prospects that oftentimes foster goodwill and relationships. These sites allow the consumers to share their opinions and leave feedback, as well as requests for help and support.

As a marketer, you can host a direct conversation with people who either have purchased your products/services or are presently searching for what you have to offer. These individuals could also be your competitors' customers looking out for a better deal, or simply wanting to be aware.

On your website, weblog, and social media profiles, customers can express their genuine thoughts and feelings about your business, particularly your brand, products, and services. You will just be more than grateful to find out having the opportune communication channels in social media to respond to their thoughts, and at the same time, to educate them.

Consumer opinions and sentiments will surely help to improve your brand to improve just as well their experiences. **Their feedbacks usually include experiences of using your products and services, general perceptions of your brand, convenience and confidence with the purchasing process, and even their opinions about the appearance, usability, and navigability of your site's interface.** With these feedbacks, you can find out if your business is truly satisfying or exceeding your customers' expectations.

Of course, your customers can leave critically negative word-of-mouth, which can amplify instantaneously or goes viral across the social media networks worldwide. Nevertheless, if your business has an adequately responsible social media marketing strategy, you can always monitor such public perceptions of your brand in real time while having the opportunity to provide effective and quick responses.

Your objective is to discover, listen to, and resolve as swiftly as possible the problems besetting your customers before these issues spin out of control. By providing them an efficient, quick, and personalized customer service, your consumers will certainly be appreciating your emphatic acts and transforming their previous feelings of antipathy into genuine sympathy.

**Vitalizing your social media customer service is also an ideal way of presenting your brand, products, and services in a more personal and interactive way.** The reality is that people are actually the ones developing, managing, and caring for all the businesses in the world, regardless of size. It is never the owners and prime movers of the business itself. All of them are seemingly puppets shaping their respective businesses in accordance with the whims and expectations of the people they serve.

Thus, such a reality makes it a necessity of highlighting the human element of your brand to your business operations. **In person-to-person conversations and liaisons online, as well as in the quick response salvations and resolutions of consumers' issues, offering a personalized experience — a human voice and a face — through a social spokesperson will certainly foster and establish the consumer's continuous engagements, trust, and loyalty in the authenticity, sincerity, and professionalism of your business.**

Apart from these intangible benefits gained from providing social customer services, interacting personally with consumers on the social media networks actually reduce indirectly your business' operational costs. For one, the supportive online community always offers their two cents' worth and pitch in a word or two of helpful answers to the posted issues on your brand. Additionally, incurred costs for every interaction in customer service and support are definitely much cheaper via the social media channels as opposed to using email support systems or the telephone.

## Cost-Effective Marketing Solution

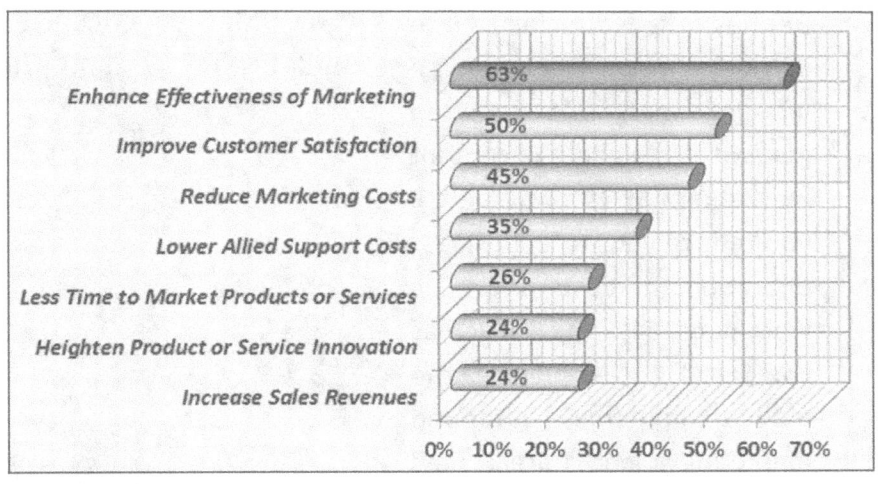

Image – 12: Benefits of Using Social Media for Business

According to the latest report from HubSpot, 63% of businesses using social media applications declared they are experiencing enhanced marketing effectiveness aside from other major benefits (refer to Image-12). It only implies the cost-effectiveness of social media marketing in several aspects of the business.

*Actually, social media marketing, as an innovative promotional tool, does not necessarily require high expenditures in advertising, much less, excessively high amounts of spending time. It has always been the ideal business strategy for marketing a brand effectively and efficiently with the least of operational costs.*

If your business is aware of where precisely to interact with your target audience on the landscape of the social media networks, then you only need a small investment, just enough to kick off a social media marketing strategy. Along the way, it would be surprising to learn that the returns are higher than you expected them to be.

Besides, if you take into account your e-commerce inbound marketing costs in general (digital content marketing, SEO, SMO, etc.), you reduce your total business operational costs by a whopping 61% per lead as compared to employing the old e-commerce outbound marketing tactic (direct mail campaigns, cold calling, ads, telemarketing, tradeshows, etc.). In short, e-commerce inbound marketing only costs 39% of outbound marketing operational costs.

*Commerce Inbound Marketing vs. Outbound Marketing*

Furthermore, the social media management platform, Social Champ, conducted its own research to distinguish precisely how social media is more affordable or otherwise. The platform tested how much would a business spend on the average by marketing for a target audience reach of 2,000 individuals through selected major marketing outlets (refer to Image-14).

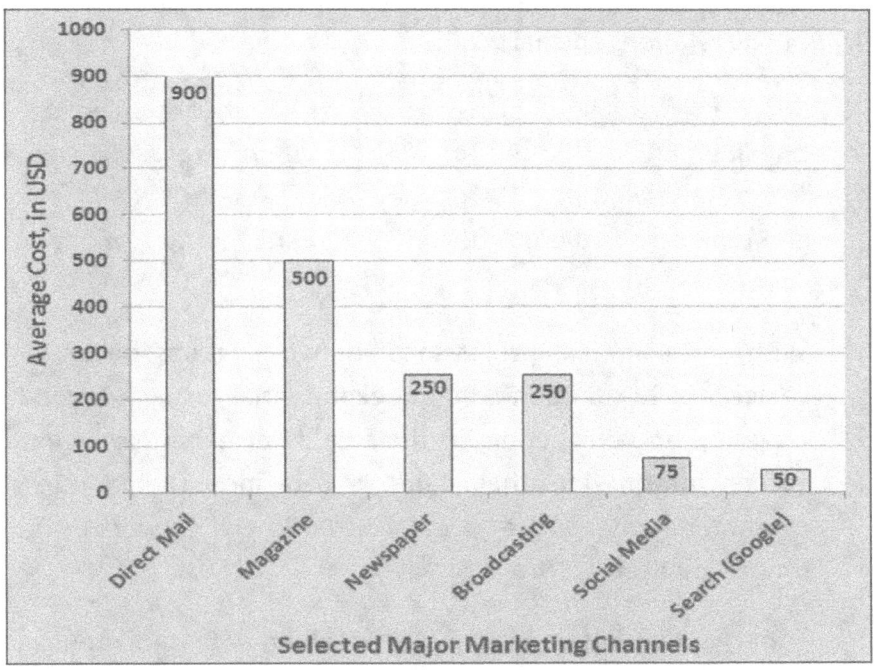

*Image – 14: Average Business Expenditures for Marketing a Reach of 2,000 Target Individuals on Selected Marketing Channels*

The results must leave business owners without doubts — an efficient, relatively low-cost, and a measured social media marketing campaign beats all other channels comprehensively. Besides, social media exhorts short-term success (i.e., increased exposure and targeted traffic) while SMO offers long-term results such as building trust-based relationships with the consumers.

# Public Relations and Social Recruitment System of Human Resources

Sales and traffic are not just about the main social media marketing benefits you should consider but also, the domains of human resources and public relations. Some of the original movers who espoused the power of social media were actually public relations specialists.

Social media and public relations are both about establishing, building, and promoting relationships. Public relations specialists use social media every single day to spread a brand's message, to communicate and engage with customers, and to respond quickly to questions or issues.

With social media, professional networking has become much easier, not to mention creating exponential results. Anybody can now link up with people in their fields of expertise or industry, gather information that helps to advance their professional career, and impress the virtual world of social networks with their professionalism.

Today, social networking indicates abilities to tap thousands of relevant connections with only a click of a button. You can even draw from the different social media channels, particularly LinkedIn, to build your professional network; or, to scout and recruit talented and able professionals; or, post your jobs alerts and connect with potential future employees. Alternatively, B2B companies can find conveniently their prospective customers from these employment- and business-oriented social networks (i.e., Linked In, ReferHire, Opportunity, Focus, Ryze, Viadeo, etc.)

Therefore, the newly developed term, *'social recruiting,'* is a defined process of businesses or employers on using social media networks as advertising and promotional platforms in recruiting their candidate employees. Social media augments and supports these systems of recruitment in several ways, as follows:

🖥 Peer-to-Peer Engagement Tracking – Social media manifests as an effective way of interacting with employees, as well as helping to monitor these peer-to-peer interactions in an efficient way. You can shortlist professionals who are currently not searching for a job transition but are tailor-made for your business, and for whom you can tap later on as the circumstances call for it.

🖥 Recruitment Facilitation – Social media assists the graduate recruitment process or searching for new candidate employees or building talent pools, by enabling you to engage with these candidates, to advertise your specific jobs, and to provide online application processes for selection.

During your hours of need, you can refer immediately to your talent pools and reach or contact those professionals who are well suited for the job to find out whether they would have interests in accepting your job offer.

🖥 Business Networking – Social media helps to build employer brand as it allows you free advertising through building your company data and profile in your profile page. Since most employees have the tendencies of posting something or another about their respective current jobs and their employers, you may as well leverage these drifts to your advantage by transforming them into your brand advocates. Through their positive appraisals and comments, your sales will certainly receive a welcome boost.

# Summary of the Social Media Marketing Benefits for Businesses

For a brief summary of this chapter, the following table (refer to Table-1) presents a structured summary of the principal benefits of social media marketing for businesses. The table organizes the benefits into the major functional areas of businesses — general marketing, social customer service, market research and development, business finance, public relations, and human resources.

| Functional Area | Benefits |
|---|---|
| General Marketing | ➢ Increased Brand Exposure<br>➢ Build Awareness<br>➢ Brand Reputation Management<br>➢ Increased Targeted Traffic<br>➢ Improved Search Engine Optimization<br>➢ Leads Generation<br>➢ Reduced Marketing Costs |
| Customer Service & Support | ➢ Customer Interaction & Feedbacks<br>➢ Real-Time And Personalized Support<br>➢ Improved Customer Experience<br>➢ Increased Customer Retention & Loyalty<br>➢ Reduced Support Costs |
| Research & Development | ➢ Market Insights On Target Audience<br>➢ Competitor Monitoring<br>➢ New Ideas Captured From Community |
| Finance | ➢ Cost-Effective<br>➢ Reduced Costs: Marketing, Customer Service, and Recruitment |
| Public Relations | ➢ Communication In Real-Time<br>➢ Increased Brand Exposure |
| Human Resources | ➢ Business Networking<br>➢ Facilitated Recruitment<br>➢ Reduced Recruitment Costs |

*Table –1: Summary of Benefits of Social Media Marketing for Businesses*

*"I use social media as an idea generator, trend mapper and strategic compass for all of our online business ventures."*

*— Paul Barron*

# Chapter 5 – The Diverse World of Social Media Networks

*"It is important to think of every customer as an online celebrity with followers, friends, & above all, influence."*

— **Dave Kerpen**

The virtual world of social media is an immense domain, which you can divide and categorize into several different types of platforms. Marketers though have each of their own specific way of distinguishing a social media channel from another.

For instance, one of the most popular models showing the various types of social media channels that people across the world are using to communicate/ interact on the Web is the annual series of illustrative social media landscapes created by the noted French web business consultant, Fred Cavazza (refer to Image-15).

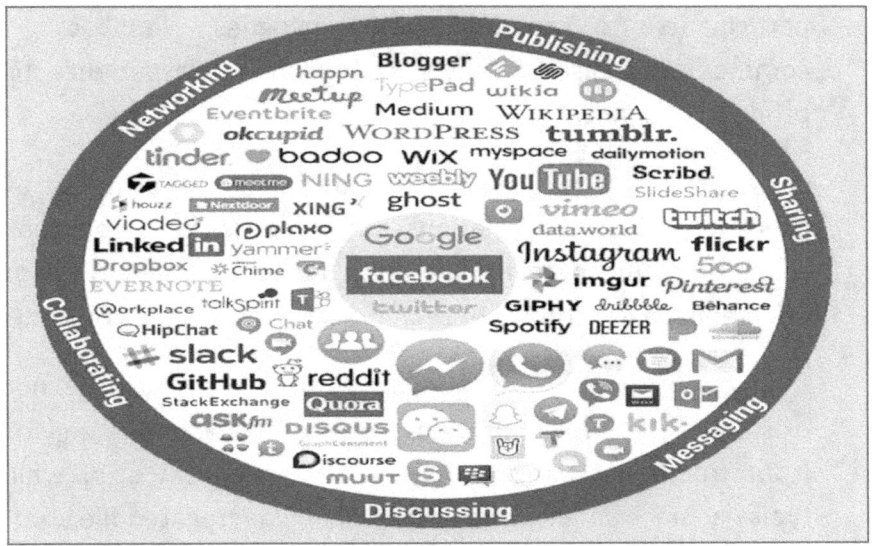

*Image – 15: Illustrative Diagram of the Diverse Social Media Landscape (Cavazza, Series 2017)*

Cavazza began spreading his annually updated series of social media landscapes since 2008 when he ultimately divided the world of social media into ten major categories:

🖥 Electronic/Online/Web/Digital Publishing – is a Web service that takes anything printable or audio/visual files and formatting these files so that it can spread and be accessible via computerized electronic devices; digital publishing includes the publication of advertisements, articles, blogs, catalogues, databases, e-books, magazines, massive libraries, newsletters, etc.

🖥 Online File Sharing – is a Web service that provides ways of storing and accessing data, documents, photos, and videos in the cloud instead of storing locally the information on a removable media or hard drive of a computer device.

🖥 Online Discussions – are communicative tools oftentimes arranging discussion boards, comment boxes, forums, and threads to extend situational conversations and learning by enabling participants to engage with dialogues, feedbacks, and commentaries based on any specific topic (i.e., experience, brand, product, or service, etc.).

🖥 Social Networking Service – is an online platform that allows users to build social relations and networks of associates who share the same personal interests, activities, career or industry affiliations, backgrounds or real-life experiences and connections.

🖥 Blogging and Microblogging – is a broadcasting medium existing in the form of blogging; wherein, a microblog only differs from traditional blogs in terms of its content size, which is typically much smaller both in actual and aggregated file size.

💻 Lifestreaming – is a Web service that allows documenting and sharing across the networks certain aspects of an individual's daily social experiences.

💻 Livecasting or Livestreaming – refers to a video live streaming channel that allows users to broadcast online live video contents in real time using a camera; viewers are able to play the content via the desktop computer or other mobile operating systems (i.e., iOS, Apple TV, Android, Roku, etc.).

💻 Social-Network Gaming – is a type of online gaming platform played typically through social networks, where the gaming console usually features multiplayer gameplay mechanics (i.e., Mafia Wars, FarmVille, Gardens of Time, etc.).

💻 Virtual Worlds – are computer-based simulated settings or environments, where users may populate, create their personal avatar, explore independently or simultaneously the environs, participate in its various activities, and interact with other users (i.e., gaming consoles, text-based chatrooms, and computer conferencing).

💻 Massively Multiplayer Online Gaming (MMO) – is an online video game played in an open or virtual world by very large numbers of interactive players, usually ranging from hundreds to thousands, under the same server (i.e., World of Warcraft, Dota 2, League of Legends, etc.).

Nevertheless, in the latest version (2017) of Cavazza's illustration of social media's diversity, the central figures in the diagram are the main pillars of the dense social media ecosystem — Facebook, Google+, and Twitter **(refer to Image-15).**

**For this reason,** it emphasizes the trio's provisions of a broad variety of functionalities and their nature of becoming relays for what users do on other social media platforms. **Furthermore, if there were any doubts about this triumvirate's supremacies, the social media diorama is much clearer today:** Facebook is undisputedly the most dominant social media platform of the 21$^{st}$ century!

Between the close to 2 billion Facebook users for its principal platform, Messenger, and the 1.2 billion WhatsApp users, and Instagram's stranglehold over Snapchat, Facebook's domination remains unchallenged, particularly among advertisers. As it is the case, the subsequent steps Facebook presumably takes to keep its number one spot are strengthening more its newly launched personal assistant, M (Messenger) and relaunching its developer platform.

**Twitter and Google+ both remain as an old couple of major players confronting Facebook's domination in today's social media scenery. Apparently,** Google shares the central domination with Twitter since it derives it gains from the mega powers of Gmail and YouTube, among others of its online properties.

**As in the case of Twitter, it surprisingly maintains its resiliency and durability despite the regular announcements of its demise.** Although Twitter is standing dwarfed alongside Facebook, it anchors its enduring strength on becoming the potent sounding board for politicians, bigwigs, and journalists. Before any further announcements of its death recur, it would be advisable to wait and see what Twitter manages to achieve with their light version app, which focuses on emerging markets and their reinvented roadmap.

Essentially, the entire diagram deals only with Western social media and without those country-focused Asian social media platforms. China may have great potentials for a large population of social media users, but their reach is limited within its borders, not to mention its government restrictions on certain social media applications.

Hence, according to Cavazza's diagram, the densely populated social media ecosystem spreads its principal services — sorted depending on usage — over the following families:

💻 Publishing – blogging engines (Blogger, Ghost, Medium, Squarespace, TypePad, Weebly, Wix, WordPress); life blog services (Posterous, Tumblr); wiki platforms or user-generated contents (Wikia, Wikipedia, Wikitravel, World66), and, social Q&A (Quora)

💻 Sharing – online services for design and inspirations (Behance, Dribbble); documents (Scribd, Slideshare); links and social bookmarking (Delicious, Digg, Diigo, Google Reader); live videos (Twitch, Periscope); music (Deezer, Pandora, SoundCloud, Spotify); photos (500px, Flickr, Giphy, Imgur, Instagram); products (Pinterest); and, videos (Dailymotion, Vimeo, YouTube)

💻 Messaging – classic messaging or webmail (Gmail, Outlook, Yahoo Mail); mobile messaging (Allo, Android Message, BlackBerry Messenger, Facebook Messenger, Google Duo, iMessage, Kik Messenger, Signal, SnapChat, Skype, Tango Telegram, Viber, WhatsApp); news aggregator (Flipboard, Google Reader); and, visual messaging (Tapatalk, Tribe)

🖥 Discussing – comment systems (Disqus, Muut, Discourse, GraphComment); collaborative FAQ (Ask, Quora, StackExchange); and, discussion platforms (4chan, Facebook, Github, Google Groups, Reddit, Tapatalk); and message boards (Phorum, phpBB, Yahoo Groups)

🖥 Collaborating – professional messaging (Chime, Facebook Workplace, Hangouts Chat, HipChat, Meet, Microsoft Teams, Slack, TalkSpirit); and, collaboration platforms (Chatter, Dropbox, Evernote, Yammer)

🖥 Networking – dating services (Houzz, Nextdoor, Ning); meeting and social events services (Eventbrite, Hi5, Meetup, Tagged, Twoo,); and, professional and career-oriented networking (LinkedIn, Plaxo, Viadeo, Xing)

Nonetheless, since this book focuses on the purposes and benefits of social media marketing for various businesses, it will exclusively analyze the social media networks that provide any direct effects or utility on businesses. Therefore, the book presents you with its own interpretative model of the list of social media channels relative to Cavazza's illustration. Specifically, this re-categorized model illustrates to interpret the connections of the communication or interactions between people, networks, and communities via the social media channels (refer to Image-16).

🖥 Social and Business Networking Sites: i.e., Facebook, LinkedIn

🖥 Blogging and Microblogging Sites: i.e., Twitter, Tumblr

🖥 Social Media Sharing Sites (Audio/Video/Photo/Content-Sharing Communities): i.e., Flickr, YouTube, Vimeo, Instagram, Pinterest

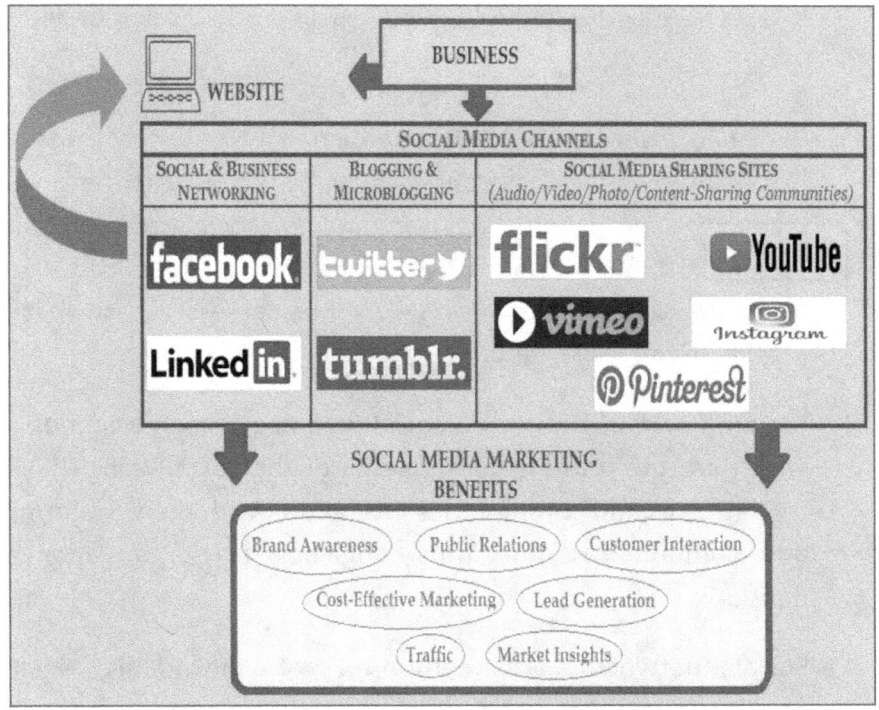

*Image – 16: Social Media Universe Focused on Social Media Channels Appropriate for Businesses and Their Brands*

Nevertheless, the challenge for businesses using social media is to find which social media channels their customers and audience spend the most and engage in conversations. Take also into account people's usual habit of *'cross-pollinating'*— visiting several social media sites rather than sticking to only a single site.

By analyzing the activities of your target audience, you can determine as to whom, when, where, and how they interact in the social media world. You can also define the influencers and their roles in online communities, whether they are daily users, networkers, reporters, trendsetters, or opinion leaders.

## Social Networks: The Primary Component of the Social Web

Businesses that market its products and services must never ignore or distance themselves away from the social networks, as well as the social web. Because people on social networks talk and share information about brands, products, and services, it makes it then a significant imperative for businesses to participate and engage in the social web.

Forming part of the entire social web are these social networks, which are the primary components of the social web. They refer to platforms and communities interacting with many other groups and communities, and thus, engaging across a wider social network.

Social networks are composed of individuals, including communities that share a common interest. Individuals frequenting these social networks never limit themselves to being a participant of any one or a couple of communities.

All these people have found the social networks to be the ideal platforms for them to participate freely and carry on a conversation in the most convenient manner. Typically, they prefer being part of the wider social network, and thus, subscribing to various networks of interest.

Concerning marketers, these are valued *'interest groups'* — communities of people sharing similar interests and working together for the protection and promotion of their interest by influencing the status quo. **Generally, these interest groups vary widely in size, goals, and tactics.**

However, they do not represent or address the entire populace at a given time, just as they are wont to do via traditional media. When they converse with one another or share their life experiences, likes, and dislikes, parts of their discussions are topics of whatever product or services they may have seen, purchased, experienced, and reviewed.

As it has always been the case to discuss certain products or services, it then becomes important, yet, urgent for that particular brand or business to listen and participate, so that it could add to the discussion certain information, clarifications, or substantiate its stand and manifestations.

For you to establish and develop your communication strategy when engaging the social web, you must first have a better understanding about all the functions, service offerings, traffic volume, components, and tools of the various social networks **(as shown in Image-16)**. For more in-depth analyses, you may also look at how business communities adopt a communication style or target the participants of each of these social networks.

You should also be able to distinguish all these sites by knowing the principal differences in terms of their respective participants and communities, as well as the pulse of these individuals. Upon learning the behaviors, expectations, and requirements of these participants, you will gain clues as to how to communicate properly with them.

You will also be able to compare the varieties and depths of information that these networks provide their members, including their breadths of subscriber coverages. In effect, you can truly identify your ideal marketing strategy to each of these sites.

## Chapter 6 – Social and Business Networking Sites

*"Networking is not about hunting. It is about farming. It is about cultivating relationships. Do not engage in 'premature solicitation.' You will be a better networker if you remember that."*

— **Dr. Ivan Misner**

Social and business networking sites are where groups of like-minded people congregate to create, recognize, or act upon personal, business, funding, as well as marketing opportunities. Among the many reasons why entrepreneurs oftentimes choose social and business networking for promoting and growing their business, is the cost-effectiveness of involving more of their personal commitment instead of company finances.

**Social and business networks promote collaboration. They can replace corporate directories and intranets (restricted company networks) and foster non-email conversation channels. Thus, they can create a forum where the discussions flourish based largely in part on the customers' experiences with the products or services that businesses promote and sell.**

Furthermore, as they gather like-minded individuals and communities around shared interests, with little to no external forces at all, they are becoming increasingly popular by each passing day due to their ability to connect people easily **worldwide.** More importantly, they contain volumes of information about prospective customers, new markets, human resources, and competitors.

Actually, they are valuable sources of lead-generation, ideas, suggestions, and target market prospecting information for marketing/advertising and sales objectives. **These sites can be either personal-oriented as** Facebook **or professional-oriented as** LinkedIn.

# Facebook

| FOUNDER(S) | Mark Zuckerberg<br>Dustin Moskovitz<br>Eduardo Saverin<br>Andrew McCollum<br>Chris Hughes |
|---|---|
| FOUNDED | 04 February, 2004 |
| WEBSITE | www.facebook.com |
| SITE TYPE | Social Networking |
| ALEXA RANK | #3 (Jan. 2018) |
| ACTIVE USERS | 2.2 billion ((Jan. 2018) |
| AREAS SERVED | Worldwide (except blocked countries) |

*Image – 17: Facebook Social Media Profile Information (2018)*

With the company's mission of, 'giving people the power of sharing and making the world more open and connected,' **Facebook is truly making the world a smaller, yet, better place for people.** In 2012, it had finally overtaken Google for being the world's most visited website or the number one social media platform, tallying one visitor for every seven minutes spent online.

Apparently, the site has gained a humongous and extremely engaged audience. It is accessible in over 70 languages, with about 75% of its monthly active users (MAU) are outside of the U.S.

**Facebook Statistics Social Media Marketers Should Know:**

💻 Usage and Preference – On the average, 1.4 billion people or 63% of Facebook's users visit the site each day. They are the site's daily active users (DAU) representing a 14%-growth year after year.

About 65% of the world's social media marketers prefer using Facebook as their primary social networking platform, with only 16% choosing LinkedIn.

That translates to more than 70 million global businesses using Facebook pages for their social media marketing strategy. In addition, 20 million business owners use Facebook Messenger to communicate with their customers.

💻 Mobile Usage – Facebook accounted about 1.75 billion mobile active users, which is a 21% growth year-over-year. Fact is that 86% of its ad revenues come directly from mobile.

However, never assume ad placements thru mobile will ever be your best option. You can determine any relative effectiveness of desktop and mobile ads for your business by applying a reliable testing protocol.

💻 Advertising – Facebook ad placements dominate over the rest of the sites. Fact is that 93% of social media marketers prefer to advertise via Facebook.

Another 64% are actually planning to increase their Facebook ad placements efforts. Currently, more than 5 million businesses around the world actively use paid advertising on Facebook.

💻 Business Returns – Facebook is the top social media platform that generates the best ROI among all the social networks according to 96.75% of global social media marketers (refer to Image-18).

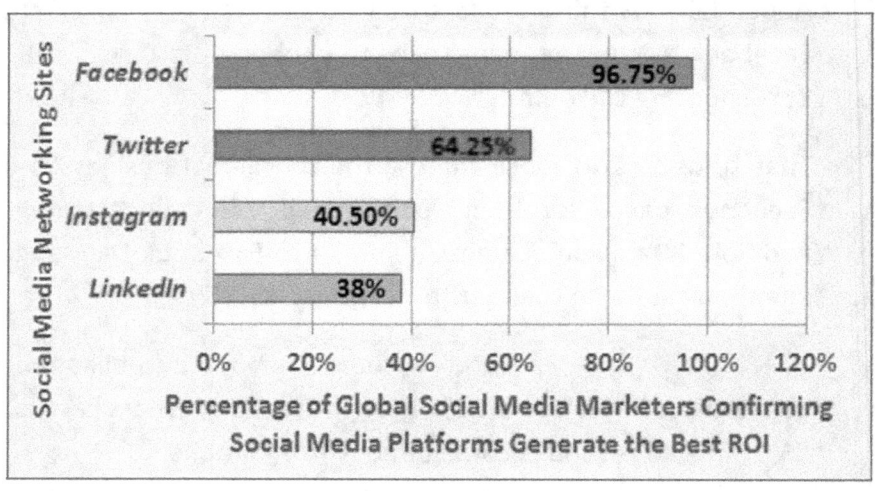

Image – 18: Leading Social Media Platforms with the Best ROI

💻 Retail Products – Facebook's own records show that 46% of its users across the U.S., European, and a few Asian countries have found fashion inspirations and guidelines on its site during the last quarter of 2017. This figure implies huge potentials in purchases of retail items in the garments business and fashion industries.

During the same period, another survey conducted by Curalate, the leading visual commerce platform, has found that 52% of their respondents were able to discover on Facebook new retail products that they were interested in purchasing. Indeed, these promising figures could benefit your plans in retail marketing (i.e., placing advertisements of your products for sale or services offered on Facebook pages.

🖥 [Schedules of Traffic Volume and Advertising](#) – Wednesdays register the highest traffic between 1 to 3 P.M (ET). However, the engagements are higher during Thursdays and Fridays, particularly during evenings.

In general, Facebook posts made at 7 P.M. (ET) lead to more clicks or views instead of posting at 8 P.M. (ET). This is the reason why Friday is the most expensive day for placing ads as opposed to Sundays and Mondays, which both have the lowest cost per click (CPC) for Facebook ads.

Throughout its years of existence, Facebook has undoubtedly manifested its potential force of helping people to communicate more efficiently. Besides, it has evolved into a powerhouse of marketing dynamics because of its broad coverage and numbers of engaged users and the simplicity of connecting with them directly, as well as its wide range of available applications.

List of Must-Have Facebook Applications:

Not all apps are tailor-fit for your business requirements. Nevertheless, when you are able to find the appropriate ones, you can save a whole lot of time for yourself by automating tedious processes in order to engage better with your customers. The following are among the brightest Facebook applications you ought to incorporate into your social marketing strategy:

💻 Photo Contests – Acquire user-generated contents while your followers or fans can share photos and vote for their top choices.

💻 Giveaways – Present a creative contest to your followers and reward winners with prizes, and at the same time, enable you to create your e-mail list.

💻 Runner Games – Offer your community a fun game and allow them to engage with great ways of competing with each other.

💻 Voters – Allow users to air their opinions by voting for the best product from a catalog of your choices.

💻 Quizzes – Ask your followers a series of questions about your brand, product or service, and reward the successful responders.

💻 Coupons – Enable your followers to print coupons and share them with their network to boost your sales revenues.

💻 Form Builder – Create any type of forms (i.e., registration, survey, order, and booking forms) easily and quickly.

💻 Web Shop – Highlights directly your brand, products, or services on your Facebook page.

💻 InstaTab – Display your Instagram account on your Facebook page to help grow your brand's visibility.

💻 TwitTab – Display your Twitter account on your Facebook page to help grow your brand's visibility.

You can also manage your presence on Facebook by using the social media management platform, Hootsuite, to schedule your posts, videos, and engagements with your followers. Additionally, the app can help you to monitor and measure the results of your marketing efforts.

Using all these powerful apps allows you to not only personalize your page but also, to gain a wider reach and be approachable, promote and grow your business, and even go viral. Try them all free today!

How to Market Your Business on Facebook:

Despite the widespread usage of Facebook by global businesses, several business owners have reported that their marketing efforts using Facebook were never as effective as they have expected it to be. Only 45% of over 3,700 surveyed marketers by the US-based media outfit, Social Media Examiner, have felt their efforts on Facebook paid them off well.

Therefore, this underscores urgencies for businesses to learn the best marketing practices worthy of pursuing a positive ROI. The following are the chief components of Facebook marketing to provide you with the best practices for each and actionable advice:

💻 Optimize Your Facebook Page to Gain 'Likes' and for SEO

| SECTION | RECOMMENDED INCLUSIONS |
|---|---|
| Category | Choose one from the list provided by Facebook |
| Sub-Categories | Select up to 3 sub-categories to better describe the business |
| Community Page | Links to any existing Facebook community page related to your Facebook page |
| Username | You can create a personalized URL after having at least 25 likes (necessary for SEO) |
| Address/City/Postcode | Provide correct information to be linked automatically with Google Map |
| Name | Name of your Facebook page (must not exceed 75 characters) |
| Creation | Date of creation of your company/business |
| About | Keyword-enhanced content for SEO purposes + links to your website |
| Description | Overview of your company or business |
| Mission | Company's mission and objectives + links to your website |
| Rewards | List of any recognized rewards received by your business |
| Products | List of the products and services offered by your business + links to your website |
| Website | Links to website and any other social media sites |
| Email | Email address for contacting your business for any further information |

*Table – 2: Recommended Best Practices of Creating Facebook Pages for Businesses*

Intents

– The opening gambit for your entire Facebook marketing efforts is your Facebook page. Ideally, ensure your page to rank in both Facebook and Google Searches in order for your prospects and customers to find your brand easily.

Moreover, your page should be appealing and sympathetic to compel people to 'like' you. Table-2 shows you the best practices of creating and optimizing your Facebook page to achieve the foregoing purposes.

💻 Boost and Promote Posts for Wider Visibility and Readership – Among the common complaints of Facebook page owners is the decreasing reach of their posts to their followers. The failure of their followers to see or read their Facebook posts actually stems from two major factors.

First, users' newsfeeds simply do not have enough space to show every post due to the sheer number of contents shared daily. This oftentimes results in a fierce competition for posts or content placements in users' feeds, and thus, a reduced exposure for organic posts.

Second, the design of Facebook's algorithm is to show the most relevant and germane contents to users' feeds. Facebook actually determines content relevancy through a slew of parameters:

➢ How a user interacted with the previous posts of a page (i.e., likes, shares, and comments);

➢ The popularity of the previous posts among all users; and,

➢ The type of post shared (i.e., image, link, video, etc.).

In short, the more popular your organic posts are, the more often will Facebook show them in users' feeds. Apply the following strategies to have the best chance of landing your posts on your followers' feeds:

➢ **Share or post videos** – Based on many research, videos have increasingly padded its lead against text-only posts in terms of organic reach.

➢ **Consult regularly with the Facebook Insights tool** – This enables you to see the types of content that influence and resonate more with users.

➢ **Ensure to include engaging and relevant backstories when posting promotional contents** – In its latest update, Facebook limits the reach of posts that are inclined to advertency or essentially too promotional.

💻 <u>Utilize Facebook Groups for Target Market Engagement</u> – **Your** participation in other business-, interest-, or industry-related groups through offering helpful tips and advice can establish your authority in your field and business. It can even prop you up as a valued member of the particular group.

Obviously, this translates to heavy traffic volumes on your Facebook page and increasing engagements with your target audience. When people grow trusting you, they will certainly be finding out more about you and your business.

Facebook Groups provide you opportunities to engage with your target audience in a more personal way. They also enable you to be a part of your target audience's day-to-day conversations.

Hence, it would be more important to create your own group page that accommodates questions, conversations, and discussions about anything concerning your business or industry, products, or services.

💻 <u>Set Appropriate Times and Frequencies of Posting</u> – **As you** would figure out the statistics on 'Schedules of Traffic Volume and Advertising' discussed previously, you can now determine precisely when to post in your Facebook page. You will have greater chances of reaching more consumers or drive heavier traffic to your business website during those cited peak usage times.

Furthermore, this helpful statistic serves as a crucial factor, especially whenever you will be planning your social communication schedules. Consider also that Facebook owns a massive global audience. Hence, you should be able to plan around the corresponding time zones of your target or key markets.

For your posting frequency, you should be able to strike a balance between annoying and informative posts. While a few businesses are successful at posting 5 to 10 times every day, it is more appropriate for other businesses to post once each day or even thrice per week.

Posting less than a couple posts a week will hardly engage your audience and keep up a regular social connection with you, and thus, dropping off their engagements eventually. Additionally, posting twice daily as a brand will also surely lose their engagements.

This denotes that the ideal posting frequency is between 5 and 10 posts weekly as a brand. As a media outfit, it is typical to post 4 to 10 times higher since news and current events are the usual staples of information people engage themselves with throughout the day.

🖥 [Promote Social Sharing Via Facebook Buttons/Plugins](#) – Synchronize your Facebook page and website. Ensure both sites to work seamlessly together. Ideally, your marketing funnel must work at driving traffic coming from your Facebook page towards your weblog or website.

Therefore, besides compelling your site visitors to interact with your content, you should provide a Facebook 'like' and 'share' buttons for each piece of content posted on your site. You may install these manually, or avail a third party service, such as the WordPress or AddThis plugin, to customize your site buttons.

Upon setting up your site's buttons, you will have options on how you want them to appear. It is highly recommendable though to choose 'Show Page Posts.' By this choice, your site visitors will have a quick preview of what type of content you usually share on your web page.

🖥 Subscribe to Paid Options for Increasing Reach and 'Likes' – Although it is possible to achieve a decent and adequate reach for your posts by using free tools, you can also supplement your campaign strategies by subscribing to paid options. At present, Facebook offers a wide variety of paid advertising options apart from boosting or promoting your post. You can readily select the type of your ad based on a list of marketing objectives (refer to Image-19).

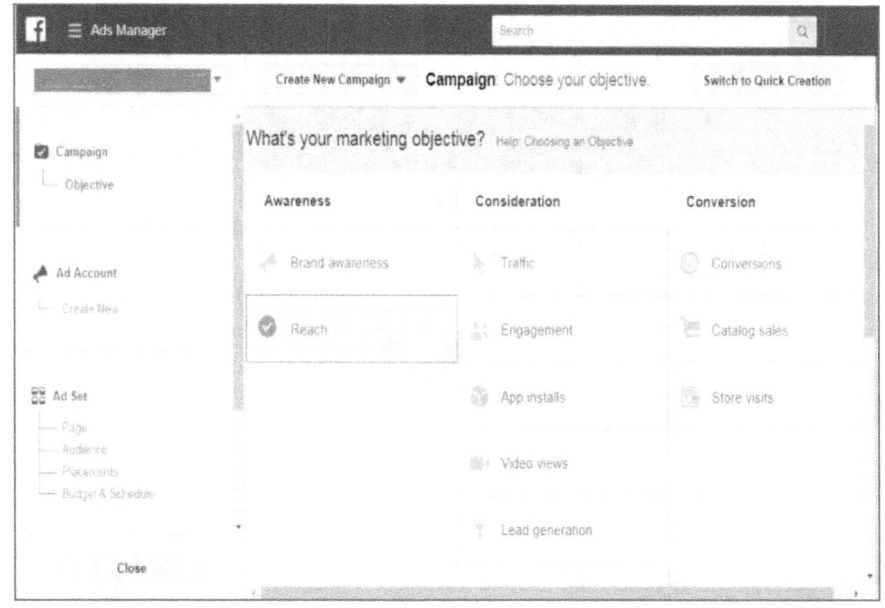

*Image – 19: Interface of the Facebook Ads Manager Tool*

➢**Promote your posts through the S.T.I.R. process – Generally, you only need to promote your posts to meet certain marketing goals such as, driving traffic to your website or selling your product.** Upon deciding on a post that you would like to promote, follow the best practice S.T.I.R. strategy for *'stirring'* or promoting a Facebook post **(refer to Image-20).**

💻 Facebook Ads Placement Best Practices – Regrettably, it is very easy to spend significant sums of money on your Facebook ad campaigns without achieving your desired marketing objectives. Just the same, ads remain effective means to gain traffic, 'Likes,' and sales conversions.

*Image – 20: S.T.I.R. Guidelines for Promoting a Facebook Post*

The following are some of the best practices that reduce your learning curve while reaching your goals quicker:

➢ Always apply audience targeting.

➢ Place your best and most important content (e.g., link or call-to-action) at the beginning of your copy.

➢ Rotate your ads week or biweekly, especially when you are applying specific audience targeting procedures. This is to avoid **'banner blindness'** or **'ad fatigue,'** which connotes decreased chances of ad visibility and click-through.

➢ Create different ads for every type of newsfeed placements (i.e., mobile, desktop, or desktop right column placement) since the display of ads appear differently corresponding to the type of users' feeds.

➢ Incorporate a strong and compelling call-to-action directive in your copy.

➢ Apply the conversion tracking pixel tool to monitor your ads that meet your goals. The tool creates a JavaScript code with an invisible 1x1-pixel image with which to place it on your ad. This unseen pixelized image will then send a notification back to Facebook when users visit or take an action.

Create your pixel by choosing from a selection of conversion types such as page views, leads, registrations, checkouts, and 'add to cart' (refer to Image-21). The Facebook Help page will guide you further for detailed instructions on how to set up the conversion pixels on your site.

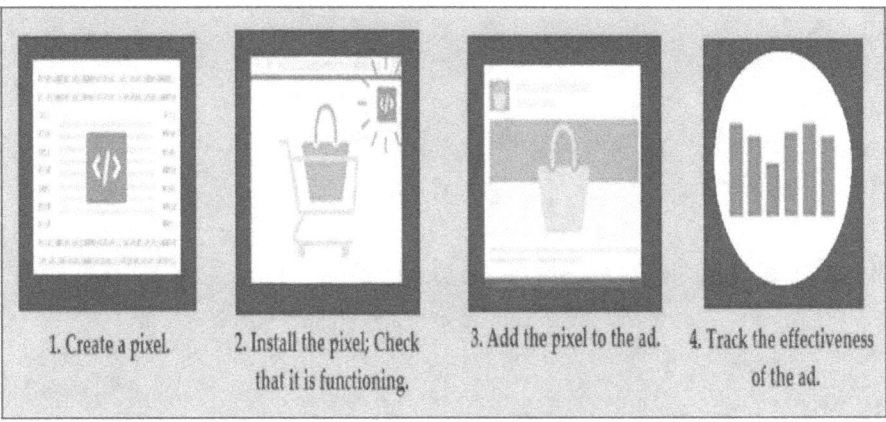

*Image – 21: Steps for Setting-Up the Conversion Pixel on Ads*

### Latest Facebook Updates in the First Quarter of 2018:

In the light of Facebook's recent updates at the outset of 2018, marketers are somehow deeply affected and feeling wary to pursue their marketing campaigns. There just seems to be an existing air of loathing marketing posts so Facebook could revert to its original cause of furthering personal connections.

Facebook overhauled its newsfeed algorithms to show more posts from family and friends of users, and fewer from publishers and promoters of businesses and brands. Specifically, Facebook discourages broadcasting typically *'promotional posts'*— posts that essentially push people to purchase goods or avail services, reuse or rehash ad contents, enter a contest, etc. **(refer to Image-22).**

*Image – 22: Facebook Founder, Mark Zuckerberg's Post about Facebook's Updates in Q1 2018*

However, the contending issue with Facebook's new strategy is that users have been actually posting lesser personal contents through the years. **Then again, the Facebook founder, Mark Zuckerberg, had emphasized clearly that the manner and time by which users engage with Facebook is about to change.**

Some points in tweaking the newsfeed algorithms are straightforward, such as posts with comments having more weight in news feeds compared to posts with a bevy of likes or shares. Yet, we are still facing a vast unknown, as well as an undetermined timeline when the updates come rolling out completely.

Being a marketer, keep on advertising. Pay closer attention towards the performance. Tweak continuously audiences. Else, in a digital world stressing the value of relationships, all you need to do is to continue emphasizing, as well, a genuine human connection.

**Although this is much easier said than done for businesses, which oftentimes exert significant efforts into enhancing communication strategies and developing Facebook communities, but only finding out in the end that their engaging and perfectly helpful content is buried,** always incline yourself to spend a portion of your digital content marketing budget on ad placements on Facebook.

It would be preposterous not to patronize Facebook ads. **For, after all, Facebook emphatically understands more about people than they truly know more about themselves, and thereby, making it a lot easier than ever to customize digital campaign ads to the right customers.**

Nonetheless, never put all your eggs in Facebook's basket. Resume having a presence on Facebook; continue building your following in order for you to advertise to your followers and to others who think and act like them. **Yet again, know that you are about to witness a declining traffic from your posts on Facebook.**

For the meantime, reconfigure and repurpose your content. Compose and blog engaging emails, and apply such copy on social media networks. Build your email list. **Email lists are treasures. You possess that data, unlike that information related to your followers via Facebook.** Grow and nurture those contacts, as they should always take precedence and priority over organic social media.

You are never alone in doubting whether you will still be going to receive the same positive or negative results for your ads expenses moving forward. Everything will be a trial and error environment as of the present. Anyway, nobody likes unknowns, especially when one is pursuing or advancing toward smart marketing objectives.

With the latest Facebook updates on clamping down engagement baits, comments will be royals. More than ever, authentic contents matter!

**Facebook can truly be an extremely effective platform for finding and engaging with your target market. When used correctly, it can result in increased traffic, reach, and conversions. Using the aforementioned best practices outlined will certainly lead you on the right path to experience all the benefits Facebook has to offer.**

## LinkedIn

Among most entrepreneurs, they easily consider LinkedIn as the most important social networking channel in terms of B2B social media— searching for jobs, connecting with investors, generating leads, or perhaps, even building a company.

| FOUNDER(S) | Allen Blue<br>Eric Ly<br>Jean-Luc Vaillant<br>Konstantin Guericke<br>Reid Hoffman |
|---|---|
| FOUNDED | 28 December, 2002 |
| WEBSITE | www.linkedin.com |
| SITE TYPE | Business Networking |
| ALEXA RANK | #31 (Feb. 2018) |
| ACTIVE USERS | 260 million (Jan. 2018) |
| AREAS SERVED | Worldwide |

*Image – 23: LinkedIn Social Media Profile Information (2018)*

Marketers perceive LinkedIn as a powerhouse with which they need to get their business visible in the eyes of executives, business peers, and professionals. The implication of LinkedIn's professional inclination is a blessing for both marketers and users alike since it only denotes less blatant and clamorous fake news, comment bots, and spam profiles, which are all more prominent in other social media platforms. In turn, this also implies that the site provides more room for noticing high-quality contents.

The widely favored professional networking channel currently boasts of having 500 million users. These users share their skills, professional history, interests, education, location, and more. Such a treasure trove of information is significant for marketers of all colors and stripes. In addition, its all-new lead generation and market targeting tools make advertising on LinkedIn more streamlined than it has ever been.

LinkedIn lives by its purpose and slogan, 'Relationships Matter,' as it continues to believe lasting relationships between people are the most valuable assets for businesses and companies. The site serves as a dynamic haven for helping both companies and individuals to achieve and sustain such relationships by allowing its registered users to build and maintain a list of contact information of people/companies, called connections.

These users' organic connections (first-degree connections) are people and businesses they know and trust in their own respective fields and industries, thus, creating a relational network of like-minded professionals. Connections are helpful for expanding or networking previous professional connections— termed as second- or third-degree connections, and for sharing news and information about their companies.

Furthermore, LinkedIn helps users to seek professional or career opportunities recommended by their connections or from listed jobs/opportunities of member companies. Equally important is the site's convenient facilitation of users to search transparently for businesses, products, and services.

**LinkedIn Statistics Social Media Marketers Should Know:**

After Microsoft Corp. entered into a $26.2B definitive agreement of acquiring LinkedIn on June 13, 2016, the already strong professional networking platform has even become stronger. Statistics show that the site has been growing steadily since its inception; and at present, no other relative professional networking sites come close to its current stature and niche.

Whether your business has not yet joined LinkedIn or your brand has already established its presence on the site, these following statistics will guide your marketing plans to create and reinforce a more effective strategy.

💻 Usage and Preference — In 2015, the social media marketing industry reported LinkedIn to have finally overtaken Facebook as the number one social networking platform for B2B marketers. At present, more than 13 million companies have already made their presence felt on LinkedIn to expand awareness for their brands.

Although a measly 21% of B2C marketers expressed the site to be their primary platform, 92% of B2B marketers placed LinkedIn at the top compared to only 30% who declared Facebook was their most significant B2B channel. Increasingly, B2B buyers keep relying on LinkedIn to advance in their journey. About 57% of them are actually on mobile devices.

💻 Lead Generation Thru Content Distribution/Advertising — While marketers spend time on other social media channels, they invest more time on LinkedIn. They search for contents that help them to solve professional issues. Thus, results are surely remarkable if your contents fit the bill. As of late, 94% of B2B marketers use LinkedIn to distribute their contents. All told, the LinkedIn feeds produce more than 9 billion content impressions per week.

High-quality contents you share on LinkedIn can also direct B2B decision makers to visit your site. On the average, 46% percent of social media traffic going back and forth to B2B sites comes from LinkedIn. However, latest studies have found 80% of B2B leads originate from LinkedIn while 43% of marketers say that they were able to source a customer via LinkedIn.

With the advanced audience-targeting capabilities of LinkedIn, you will have the assurance that an increased traffic volume contains entities that will most likely convert into leads. Proof of this is the testimony of 79% of B2B Marketers attesting LinkedIn is the most effective source for lead generation.

💻 Schedules of Posting and Sharing of Contents – Tuesday is the best day to post your content on Linked for engagement. Specifically, posting time should be between 10 and 11 A.M. (ET). Alternatively, the best time to post for the purposes of compelling users to share your content is between the hours of 10 A.M. and 2 P.M. (ET).

The number of posts that it takes to reach at least 60% of your LinkedIn audience is 20 posts per month. Therefore, you need not post daily to target a 90% reach. Just imagine the exponential results you get when connections share your great contents.

**List of Must-Have LinkedIn Applications:**

It is noteworthy that LinkedIn has unfolded a number of useful products and applications to promote your personal work or business better. It does not actually matter what industry you are in; LinkedIn offers an application for everyone that helps you to make your message more convincing and understandable and enhance the general experiences of your profile. Go to the 'Work' section on your profile **(refer to Image-24)** to access and see which applications you could use.

**Nevertheless, digital strategist and top global LinkedIn/email marketing expert, Nathan Kievman, is recommending to all LinkedIn users to add at least a single application, but not more** than five apps, to stave off the clutter in your profile space. Hereunder are top five applications that are worthy to explore and use to your advantage:

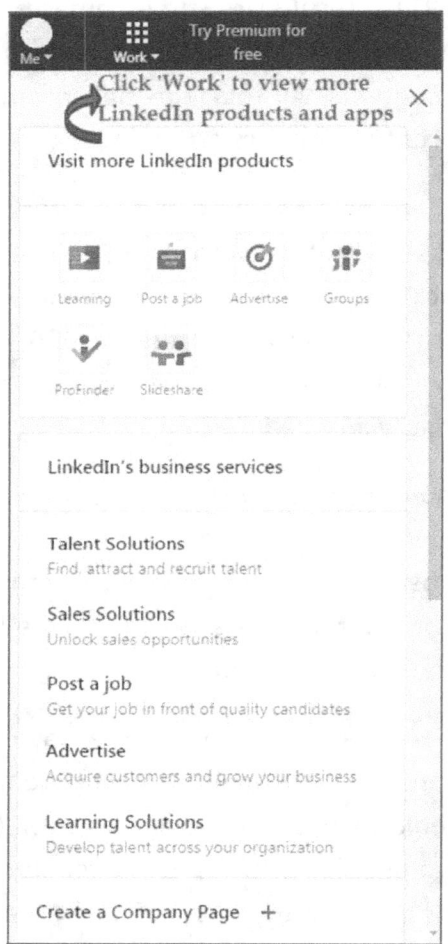

*Image – 24: List of LinkedIn Products, Services, and Applications under the 'Work' Menu of the Profile Page*

💻 Company Buzz — This tool enables you to aggregate mentions of companies from Twitter. Thus, it helps you to discover relevant comments and pertinent trends about your business or target audience. **You can modify and customize what topics to watch out, trends to monitor, or selected charts and infographics (that track business activities) to display.**

💻 Reading List by Amazon — Amazon's Reading List allows you to use a search tool to create a book collection, which you have read or reading right now or yet to read. You will have three lists of books to view using this application: one coming from connections in your field, from people in your business and from those updates detailed on LinkedIn.

You can follow others' reading list, just as others can follow yours. This is a valuable application for finding out what books must be on your list, discovering books recommended by your connections, as well as growing and fostering goodwill relationships with people.

💻 WordPress — When you are maintaining a blog via WordPress, you can synchronize automatically all your posts with your LinkedIn page. You can also filter your posts or select only those entries fit for sharing with your connections.

The same goes when sharing your posted tweets on LinkedIn. You should exercise caution on which posts are only appropriate to share and how frequent you should share them.

💻 Events — This application places a box on your profile showing the events your connections will be attending. You can also find events fit for you based on your field and the nature of your job.

Moreover, you can view details of the most popular events, search for relevant events, as well as create new ones by using this app. Its significance is more inclined in building and expanding your connections prior to following up or attending conferences, webinars, etc.

💻 SlideShare Presentations – You may also sign up for a SlideShare account thru the 'Work' tab on your LinkedIn profile page. If you are already a SlideShare user, you can post or share your documents, presentations, infographics, etc. to your LinkedIn page.

Using this app, you can browse and view from a list of SlideShare presentations uploaded by your connections. You can also watch presentations of *'Featured SlideShares'* and *'Featured Courses from LinkedIn Learning,'* discover and click through the most downloaded presentations and search for the latest webinars, conferences, and business trends.

**How to Market Your Business on LinkedIn:**

Currently, freelancers, established companies, digital creatives, professionals, and even performing artists in the world of entertainment use LinkedIn to promote their brands, products, and services with an audience other than what is generally available in other social networks.

Facing now a different audience, correct branding is the key to finding the right leads or biz partners on LinkedIn. In short, it is taking the approach with a smart marketing strategy. The following are helpful tips to give your presence and marketing efforts with a more solid traction on LinkedIn:

💻 <u>Create Your Company or Brand Page</u> — Compared to personal profiles, setting up a company page on LinkedIn is to represent better an organization or brand. It is always a prudent move to use a company page and connect it with your LinkedIn personal profile even if you manage a small business operation. The page enables you to add information and post updates that get across much better coming from a brand name rather than from an individual.

💻 <u>Put Strong Emphases on Your Business on Your Own Profile Page</u> — A personal profile page remains a powerful instrument on LinkedIn. It provides you with opportunities for building your professional reputation and presenting yourself as the person behind your brand. Ensure to include important activities of your business, as well as links to all the significant pages in your profile details such as your professional Twitter account, business website or weblog, etc.

💻 <u>Update Frequently Your Profile and Company Pages</u> — Keep on informing strategically your professional community by posting news on the recent developments of your business. These pertinent updates should include new collaborations or cooperation, recently completed projects, news coverage, novel products or features, creative tips, and anything that can highlight the dynamism and serious operations of your business.

💻 <u>Apply Great Visuals</u> — Although LinkedIn is not a known network that uses visuals, just take advantage of the available freedom you have with images. Each type of visual content uploaded should be of high quality— from your own profile picture to your company logo. For example, when posting updates, you may edit the images shown with it.

🖥 <u>Engage People by Starting a Group</u> – Groups are social features on LinkedIn that allows you to set up one, which revolves around a certain topic or specific interest. Connect your business to topics that engage people. Ensure that group members know about your business, and stir a discussion with them.

🖥 <u>Participate in Other Groups</u> – Aside from creating your own community, you ought to join and be active in other communities by interacting with other users. **Lest misinterpreting the intent of spamming these groups with your posts on your business activities,** the idea here is to engage in actual conversations that build genuine relationships.

🖥 <u>Involve Employees and Business Partners in Your Activities</u> – Working under an environment of team efforts and collaboration with other professionals will gain more attention, especially when you involve the team participants in your LinkedIn activities. As strangers browse your company page followed by these skilled and experienced professionals, your credibility grows quickly.

🖥 <u>Write Your Contents Smartly</u> – You should target and optimize your posted contents, including texts on your profile page, company updates, and company information section. A couple of significant factors to consider are to use keywords emphasizing your field of expertise and writing curt and concise contents highlighting your authority in your industry.

🖥 <u>Always Interact</u> – While LinkedIn focuses more on a professional aspect, it is still essentially a social network. Hence, you always need to be social, by engaging yourself with people. Fortunately, LinkedIn shows you circles of connectivity to guide you towards interacting with the right people.

You can browse through the profiles of your connections. Find out to whom they are involved with and their allied associations. You can certainly discover valuable leads through these pages.

💻 [Participate on LinkedIn Actively and Seriously](#) – **Exert extra efforts towards understanding how LinkedIn can work best for you. Just like with any other social media platform, LinkedIn only works well for you if you are active and serious about your participation.**

Since it is not a social network for all the masses, several people usually fall into using LinkedIn in a slapdash manner. To earn real results, you must integrate LinkedIn into your comprehensive social media marketing strategy.

**Stay updated on LinkedIn's news or your network. Keep on learning about its tools, features, apps, and products. You may also browse through personal profiles and company pages to witness how others are leveraging LinkedIn to their favor.**

> "A brand is no longer what we tell the consumer it is – it is what consumers tell each other it is."
>
> — **Scott Cook**

## Chapter 7 – Blogging and Micro-Blogging Sites

*"Blogging is not for earning. It is about helping others with the knowledge you have."*

— **Syed Faizan Ali**

Blogs are web pages where people post reviews, comments, or write about certain topics and share the information on the Web. They are essentially journals published online.

Typically, they consist of entries— termed as posts— and usually shown in a reversed chronological order so that the latest post appears first. Blogs, in general, are free, accessible, easy to use, interactive, personal, and includes multimedia.

In addition, blogs bring forth credibility to the basic website of a business and provide a more personal interaction with the target audience. Nonetheless, creating and maintaining a popular blog is certainly a full-time job.

Besides, it can be time-consuming, especially when creating contents for regular publication while moderating the comments section and responding as quickly and efficiently as possible to the queries or requests of readers. Yet, most of the time, companies employ the services of professional bloggers to create contents in accordance with the social media plans designed by the company.

For several businesses, these blogs, used for the purposes of branding, marketing, and promoting in public, are technically **'external corporate blogs.'** Writing corporate blogs are primarily for other businesses or consumers.

These type of blogs are generally trying to achieve the same objectives as press releases, regardless whether they can be less formal or not. Hence, they can explain business policies, announce the launchings of new brands, products, or services, or present valuable information about the business' industry.

Initially, bloggers began writing blogs as single author pages. Nevertheless, professional blogging has evolved with the changing times.

It has actually come of age, whereby, multiple authors contribute and write to the blogs of various topics and subjects. With this trending shift of writing blogs from single to multiple authors, it only means producing more enhanced contents with high qualities of discussions.

Previously, blog posts only used to contain text messages. Nowadays, professional blogs contain audio, video, and image clippings, etc., which all makes it interesting and an enriching experience for readers. As a marketer, use to your advantage such blogs for your ad campaign and online brand building.

The social media industry refers to the blogging community as *'blogosphere'*. Like websites, blogs can contain blogrolls (sets of links), backlinks, and other significant features that enable their interconnection and networking with one another.

You may find blogs in almost all scopes— personal, business related, professional, research, academic, etc. In fact, blogs coming from the academe, research, and other interest-based groups are steadily on the rise.

A wide selection of blog search engines is available for use whenever you want to search for blogs on various subjects. Among these search engines, BlogScope and Technorati are the most popular. They provide blog searchers with options for looking the more popular and recent tags used in blog posts.

Additionally, you can source the best blogs from international communities of bloggers, writers, digital activists such as Global Voices and BlogCatalog. **However, the intentions of these online communities are translating and reporting on what the global citizen media says. They also provide you with connections to several groups and multiple bloggers.**

All told, blogging is worth trying. Blogs provide contents that are interactive, which leads to catch the attention of the search engines and gain the best rankings for SEO. In effect, blogs ranking high on the SERPs enhance the volume of traffic to the company's website. The same goes for improving its brand awareness.

**Furthermore, blogs that are active on Facebook, Twitter, and other social media sites heightens the chances for improved rankings of the company's website.** Yet, it is always important to test or evaluate the effectiveness of the blog posts and to know how they reached the target audience.

Such evaluations would let you know which of your posts are most appropriate for a wider audience reach and readership. More importantly, you will know the proper frequency of posting and publishing since blogging frequency influences greatly the acquisition behaviors of customers. Truly, producing more business blogs also produces the acquisition of more customers.

The World Wide Web today contains over 175 million blogs. This speaks of volumes about the popularity of blogs as a networking channel. Thus, each management student and marketing manager shall have to take time going through different types of blogs and have a better understanding about all of them.

*Foremost, marketers should be able to recognize the theme of the blog, approximate the volume of posts, observe the pattern of posts and comments (i.e., their tones and the setup of holding, organizing, and moderating the discussions), and feel the pulse of the target audience.* With such a comprehensive understanding about blogs, it will give you an idea of how to use this platform effectively for social media marketing. The following blogging statistics can further help you to design your campaign strategies (refer to Image-25).

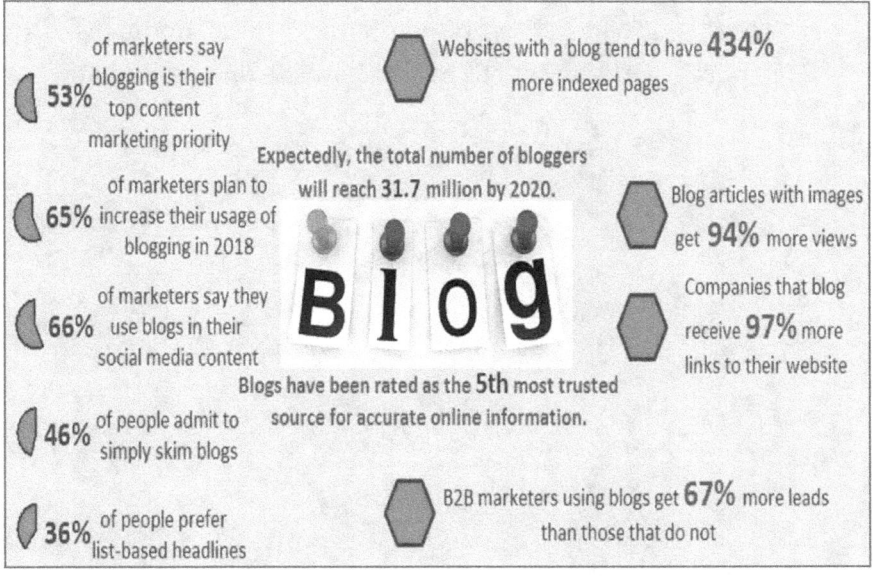

*Image – 25: 2018 Blogging Statistics Every Marketer Should Know*

For further significant information about blogging, you should include some types of visuals in your blog since 71% of marketers have reported that the application of visual assets reaped favorable traffic results in their digital content marketing strategies. **Always enhance your blog entries to look more appealing; for, after all, blog articles influence directly purchases.**

The classical blog typically averages a total word count between 400 and 1,000. However, the average length of top-ranking contents in Google Search ranges from 1,140 to 1,285 words. Obviously, the usual microblog posting has much lesser words.

**When posting your blog entries or sharing links and commenting on blogs, bear in mind that the most popular time for reading them is in the morning.** More people tune in during the day, and they usually frequent the following established microblog channels— Twitter, Tumblr, and the status update feature of Facebook— out of the 111 microblogs existing worldwide.

# Twitter

| **twitter** | |
|---|---|
| FOUNDER(S) | Jack Dorsey<br>Noah Glass<br>Biz Stone<br>Evan Williams |
| FOUNDED | 21 March, 2006 |
| WEBSITE | www.twitter.com |
| SITE TYPE | News/Microblogging |
| ALEXA RANK | #13 (Jan. 2018) |
| ACTIVE USERS | 330 million (Jan. 2018) |
| AREAS SERVED | Worldwide |

*Image – 26: Twitter Social Media Profile Information (2018)* messaging service online based on the 160-character short message service (SMS) software system for text messaging. For this reason, no one has actually had the time or a longer attention span to read more than a few sentences. Since then, it has grown to become the most popular blogging and microblogging social media site, as well as an online news service system. Twitter allows users to post and interact with messages (known as *'tweets'*) containing only 140 characters or less.

However, on November 7, 2017, Twitter doubled the character limit of its messaging system to 280 characters for all the world's major languages except for the Chinese, Korean, and Japanese (CJK) glyphs or characters, which counts as two characters. Thus, only 140 such CJK glyphs are permissible in a tweet.

Initially, Twitter was not clear what it really was. There were no standard ways on Twitter for replying or tracking interesting discussion and conversations on a given subject. People and Twitter themselves had called the site a social network; others termed it as a microblogging activity. Yet, it was difficult to define, since it never replaced anything.

It is no wonder why its slogan says, 'Yours to Discover.' There seems to be an existence of a likely path of discovery with something as such: where, in the passing of time, you come to figure out what it truly is.

Actually, Twitter had changed from what people perceived it was at the start, described simply as a social utility for status updates. In essence, the status updates, in part, made the social platform to be inclined more to an information network rather than exhibiting the nature of a social network.

When users re-post a message or tweet from another user so they can share the post with their followers, they simply click the 'retweet' button of the source tweet. Additionally, users can categorize posts together by type or topic through using *'hashtags'*—words/phrases prefixed with a *'#'* symbol.

In the same fashion, the *'@'* symbol followed by the username is for citing or replying to other Twitter users. This twin messaging tools denote a more dynamic development of conversation threads while involving more communities of similar interests on the message or topic. However, as part of the character-count change, Twitter also limited its hashtag length to 100 characters.

*'Trending topics,'* consisting of a word or phrase or topic cited at a much greater rate than other topics, become popular due to either the concerted user efforts or any events that prompt people to talk about a certain subject.

Twitter displays the current list of trending topics, along with some sponsored contents, on the sidebar of a home page. These topics help users to learn and understand what is presently happening in the world and the most pressing opinions of people about them are.

Twitter shares some common features with the most popular social media sites (Facebook, LinkedIn, Pinterest, and YouTube). Nevertheless, the differences really define Twitter.

Versus Facebook, a tweet is similar to a brief Facebook status update. Yet, with Twitter, each tweet appears at the feed of every follower. Facebook filters some updates through its EdgeRank filtering tool.

Versus LinkedIn, a tweet is similar to a brief LinkedIn status update. LinkedIn bases connections on trust relationships or two-way agreements); Twitter enables you to follow anybody, including strangers. This becomes helpful, especially when you are targeting potential leads and customers.

Versus Pinterest, Twitter allows you to share images and provide commentaries in your tweets. Hence, it is much easier having conversations around a shared photo as opposed to the comment feature that Pinterest has.

Versus YouTube, a tweet may contain a link to a certain video. Yet, Twitter prohibits you to create your own channel where you can organize your videos for convenient access and commentary.

**Twitter Statistics Social Media Marketers Should Know:**

💻 Usage and Preference – A combined 66% of users access the Twitter channel at least weekly, with 42% of them using the app daily while another 24% use the network on a weekly basis. Despite its popularity though, not everyone uses the app.

The average user only has 27 followers while a quarter of all Twitter accounts never had any followers and 40% of these accounts never sent or posted any tweet.

The specific societal segment of Twitter users composes of young, tech-savvy, smart, educated, and affluent people. Additionally, these people spend more time online, thus, tending to be early adopters. About 35% of Twitter MAU is between the ages of 25 and 34 years old. Nevertheless, more than 50% of them are ardent followers of businesses, brands, or products on other social media networks.

💻 Mobile Usage – At the latest estimates, 80% of users access the Twitter on the go or on mobile devices. Fact is that 93% of video views on Twitter happen on mobile.

💻 Advertising Engagement – Twitter's figures show that the overall ad engagements have been steadily increasing at the rate of 99% year-after-year, as last recorded in Q4-2017. The continuing shift towards a combination of video ad impressions and higher click-through rate (CTR) across all ad formats on a like-for-like criterion had spurred such increased ad engagement activities.

Bearing all these Twitter statistics in mind, you are now well equipped to design your specific Twitter marketing plan that can allow your business to be in front of new Twitter users, make the most of your responses to your paid and organic tweets, and increase the engagement with users who matter most to your brand.

💻 Amplification of Message – Twitter users have strong tendencies of amplifying your messages. More than 33% of Twitter users who are SMB followers have 'retweeted' business tweets. Tweets with videos actually receive more retweets than any other form of tweets.

Tweets containing videos are 6 times more prone to retweeting compared to tweets with only photos in them. Additionally, video tweets are thrice more possible for retweeting against tweets with graphics interchange format (GIF) files. With these relative statistics, you can then deduce that tweets with GIF files are twice as likely to undergo amplification or retweeting as tweets with photos.

💻 Business Returns – Twitter has become the ideal platform for small and medium business (SMB) enterprises, with 44% of SMB marketers attesting to having acquired leads from Twitter. Additionally, 69% of people following SMB entities on Twitter have already purchased items or services from these SMBs.

What is rosier is the fact that 93% of SMB followers are planning to purchase more from these business enterprises. About 85% of (SMB) Twitter users have declared that it is more than necessary for their operations to implement their respective customer service programs through the app.

This gave rise to the 57% of businesses in social media to use the services of Twitter. These businesses are taking advantage of Twitter's real-time news feed by applying it as their effective customer service outlet and news or information-broadcasting tool. In fact, 83% of people who have tweeted at an SMB and eventually got a response left feeling better about the business.

💻 Search Queries – Twitter serves over 2 billion search queries daily. Generally, an increased 74% of Twitter users use the channel to get their daily news and current events not only on the present political landscape but also in the lifestyle, fashion, retail, and entertainment scenes.

List of Must-Have Twitter Applications:

It is never a breeze for freelancers or small business enterprises to make a bright business sense out of Twitter! Foremost, using Twitter for social media marketing usually demands certain indispensable tasks that you should be performing on a regular basis.

Among these crucial tasks are managing tweets; building your lists; knowing whom to follow; having a single overview for all the conversations relating to your business; or, simply managing your business' Twitter account across different people. Here is a shortlist comprising of the best Twitter apps and tools to assist you in managing your account efficiently.

💻 Hootsuite (Best app to monitor your Twitter activities)

💻 Cotweet (Best app for your brand management)

💻 ManageFilter (Best app for managing actively your followers)

💻 OneForty (Best tool for searching new Twitter apps)

💻 Seesmic (Best app for managing your multiple social media accounts)

💻 SocialOomph (Best tool for your social media automation)

💻 SproutSocial (Best dashboard for managing your social media accounts)

💻 Streamie (Best curation tool for digesting only the most significant tweets)

💻 Tweello (Best directory for your Twitter account)

💻 TwitIQ (Best tool for your Twitter analytics)

In addition, you can check out other important Twitter or business apps and tools that are strongly compatible with Twitter integration like DemandSpot for your lead generation; Assistly for customer service or as a help desk; or, CoWorkers for receiving professional feedback from peers and associates.

Twitter is indeed a massive universe, where you may waste a huge amount of your time. Therefore, you just need to use all these aforementioned apps on Twitter, as well as with all your other social media accounts, in a productive way.

How to Market Your Business on Twitter:

Regardless of what has occurred or will occur, you will most likely consider taking a fresher look at the new offerings of Twitter, including its latest updates, real-time marketing, and trends in multi-screen usages. Take using Twitter for your business to the next level to achieve your business objectives. Here are the most important basics to inspire you in marketing your business on Twitter:

💻 Master the Following Twitter Skills —Here is a checklist of everything your business needs to do to get on (or back on) Twitter and start seeing great results.

➤ Present your business, brand, product, or service. – Optimize your profile page to tell a story about your business. Select your account username. Upload your profile images— profile and background photos.

➤ Establish and build a solid foundation. – Fill out your account profile completely. Twitter offers the following features to provide more info on your business and contribute to your story:

❖ Bio – You have only 160 characters to relate to people who you are, what you do, and what benefits does your business delivers.

❖ Location – Tell and give people sufficient information to where they can find you.

❖ **Website** – Share your weblog or website with your community.

➢ Begin following people. – **Follow people falling under these categories: customers; business associates/partners, vendors suppliers, and contractors; business colleagues, peers, or competitors; professional or trade organizations of your industry; business located in your community; and businesses operated by your professional network or the people you know. Twitter will be assisting you to find people you know through your email address book.**

➢ Start conversing. – **Conversing on Twitter is much different from other social media networks. It is a fast-paced miscellany of ideas, colloquialisms, and sentence fragments. It may be feverish, but it is also a lot of fun. Twitter offers the following types of messages that you can apply to your advantage: tweet, @reply, mention, direct message (DM), and retweet.**

➢ Converse smartly. – **It is an art to write a headline-style tweet with only 280 characters to get your message across. Generally, look for the sweetest spot between the aspects that promote your business and what your target market really wants to hear. Focus on how your brand, product, or service will benefit your customers. At the same time, you should also provide your audience with useful information and respond to each of their questions in a more transparent, personal, and emphatic way.**

➢ Compel to drive traffic to your weblog or website. – **Create your tweet around a specific link by writing a message that can compel people clicking to learn or ask for more. Since space is restricted in a tweet, you will surely have no room to include the** entire web address. Your Twitter URL tool, however, will enable you to shorten your web addresses within just 20 characters.

➢ Synchronize your online presences. – Integrate your Twitter account into your entire presences of your business online. Add the information to your Twitter account to the social media account details section on your website or weblog. Add also to your website the timeline of your Twitter posts. Always make it convenient for people to share your blog or web page contents on Twitter.

➢ Connect via mobile. – Jump on the bandwagon of using mobile devices and services. Using the Twitter app with your smartphone can let you send and receive tweets easily. Even non-smartphones with an SMS texting service can allow you to use Twitter by creating text messages.

➢ Share high-quality images in your tweets. – This may be a no-brainer since people always love to see pictures. Thus, serve their inherent desires by affixing photographs in your tweets.

➢ Contribute videos to your timeline. – Videos are powerful alternative ways of relating your business to people. Besides, people will most likely watch your videos as manifested by the statistics aforementioned. While you can add videos to your timeline, Twitter has no capabilities of adding them directly. You should upload them first to another video service platform such as YouTube or Vine, and then, link these videos in your tweet.

➢ Categorize your followers into conversation lists. – While you are following more people, focusing on the information tweeted from certain people or groups can be challenging. Thus, the

Twitter List becomes helpful by allowing you to categorize into specific groups all the accounts you follow. Organize your list in a manner that helps you and your business.

➢ Expand the reach of your target audience by using hashtags. – Create a hashtag that is unique and exclusive to your business. Use it in your marketing efforts (i.e., conferences, webinars, etc.) in helping people to find your business and the entailing conversations around it. Fact is that hashtags are great means of using Twitter for purposes of customer service and support.

➢ Nail down potential leads and local customers. – Although it is a fact that the common perception of people about social media is allowing you to connect outside of your geographical location, among the greater strengths of Twitter is its capability of focusing on probable connections or potential customers right in your own backyard. Of course, you need local customers. You can use the Twitter Advanced Search feature to help you locate people who are near your business locale.

🖥 Evaluate Your Twitter Performance. – It is much easier and convenient to achieve better marketing results when you have concrete data about how your Twitter strategies are faring. Use the Twitter Analytics to measure your campaign performances.

🖥 Concentrate On Building Your Community of Twitter Followers. – Many tools (i.e., Commun.it, inboxQ, Tweriod + Buffer, ClickToTweet, Brandfluencers, etc.) allow you to review who your followers are and to reach out to your target market.

🖥 Know Which of Your Tweets or Links Are the Most Effective with Your Audience. – Use Twitter tools to create a split test for your tweet to determine periods on when your followers are most active or which tweet really receives a better response. This will also help you to determine when you should publish your future tweets to reach the largest and most engaged audience. You can also use Bit.ly to create a split test for your link.

🖥 Expound Your Conversation Topics. – **Enhance** your tweets by adding more variety (i.e., daily deals, promos, events, hashtags, guides, case studies, etc.) to your conversation topics to draw in more engagements from your target audience.

🖥 Tweak Your Presence To Gain Better Results. – **When** noticing a slump in your performance, create the necessary updates and adjustments that can contribute to your solid presence on Twitter.

# Tumblr

| | |
|---|---|
| **tumblr.** | |
| FOUNDER | David Karp |
| FOUNDED | 19 February, 2007 |
| WEBSITE | www.tumblr.com |
| SITE TYPE | Microblogging |
| ALEXA RANK | #54 (Nov. 2017) |
| ACTIVE USERS | 116 million (Jan. 2018) |
| AREAS SERVED | Worldwide |

*Image – 27: Tumblr Social Media Profile Information (2018)*

Tumblr's microblogging and social networking website services allow its users to post multimedia and other contents to a *'tumblelog'* (short-form blog). Bloggers access many of the site's features from its dashboard interface.

The posting and management of blogs in Tumblr revolve around five basic aspects: dashboard, queueing, tagging, and hypertext markup language (HTML) editing.

The dashboard is the chief tool for the Tumblr user. It serves as your live feed of the latest posts from other blogs you follow. Using the dashboard, you can comment, re-blog, or like the posts from other blogs appearing on it.

Furthermore, the dashboard enables you to upload images, text posts, quotes, videos, audios, or links to your own blog. Tumblr also allows you to connect your blog with your Facebook and Twitter accounts; hence, whenever you post anything on Tumblr, it sends the post simultaneously as a status update and a tweet.

With queueing, you can set up your preferred schedules for delaying the broadcasting of your posts. Thus, you can spread out your posts over certain periods; say, hours, or even, days.

Tagging helps your target audience to find posts about particular topics through affixing tags. Thus, you only have to add the "#" symbol and type a keyword or key phrase of your post.

Using Tumblr's HTML editing tool, you can edit the HTML coding of your blog's theme to manipulate its appearance. You can also use a customized domain name for your blog.

**Tumblr Statistics Social Media Marketers Should Know:**

Somehow, Tumblr is still a relatively unknown entity since its inception. Perhaps, it is because Tumblr has not yet gone public or listed itself on the stock exchange. With its present owner, Oath, Inc., it remains a subsidiary of Verizon Communications.

As such, it is not necessary for the company to release statistics periodically. Nevertheless, these following statistics gathered from around the Web will help you to decide whether Tumblr is suited for your business.

🖥 Usage and Preference – Tumblr receives more page views coming from a desktop computer browser than from browsers of mobile devices. Computers at home visit the site more than computers at the workplace. The average Tumblr user spends only 20 to 25 minutes on the site per visit.

🖥 Users/Audience – The general audience of Tumblr is among the youngest, where 45% are below 35 years old. Fact is that it is more popular than Facebook with people aged 13 to 25 years old. Being so, only 33% of its users have children.

About ⅔, or 65% of the users, bear a college education. Male users only comprise 47% of the total users. The US, UK, Brazil, Russia, and Canada compose the top five countries using Tumblr, with African-Americans and Hispanics making up 29% of its regular users.

🖥 Business Returns – The microblogging site has been able to attract a monthly average of more than 300 million unique visitors with a little over 5 billion monthly page views in 2014. These visitations converted to annual revenues of only a little less than $30,000 for 35% of Tumblr users.

Actually, Tumblr's average revenue per visit (RPV) amounts to $1.10. Record-wise, this amount represents the second highest RPV for all social media sites, tailing closely Facebook, which registered at $1.22.

As the statistics show, it only means that Tumblr is the social media watering hole of the youth. Therefore, Tumblr definitely is where your business needs to be when you are marketing products or services for young adults, or even college students. Alternatively, it would not be the ideal site for you to market expensive or luxury products since with 35% of users were only earning less than $30,000 a year, or roughly, $2,500 a month.

**List of Must-Have Tumblr Applications:**

 Tumblr Mobile Apps – Spicing up your Tumblr experience and equipping yourself to tumble with the same functionalities of the web application (except for video posting) while on the go would be availing the following apps for mobile devices: Tumble (iPhone Tumblr App), BlackBerry Tumblr, and Atumble (Google Android Phone App).

 Tumblr Web Apps – Tumblelog and Hellotxt are two significant apps for your business when using Tumblr. **Tumblelog, which is a Facebook app, places your Tumblr blog in a tab on your Facebook profile. It broadcasts automatically your blog posts in your Facebook news feed so your friends can view it without even visiting your Tumblr profile.**

Hellotxt is essentially a productivity tool. It allows you to save precious time by updating completely, all at once, all of your social media networking sites, email, or third-party apps.

💻 Tumblr Website and Browser Tools — You also have a couple of significant apps for your Tumblr site and browser— Tumblr Post and Tag Cloud Generator. **Tumblr Post, a Firefox add-on, lets you blog with an easy drag-and-drop function to your status bar.**

Tag Cloud Generator is a free, convenient, and copy-and-paste tool for a string of lines of HTML to generate a tag cloud for your blog, thus, making it live and interactive. When using tags more frequently, they will appear larger than the seldom-used tags, providing your new viewers some ideas about what your content is focusing (refer to Image-28).

*Image – 28: Sample Illustration of an Interactive Tag Cloud*

**How to Market Your Business on Tumblr:**

Admittedly, marketers rarely acknowledged Tumblr as an important social media network. Usually, they prefer using the leading sites like Facebook, Twitter, Instagram, and Pinterest. Lest you are not sure of how to market your brand using Tumblr, you just need to know about the bright opportunities Tumblr has to offer with your business.

Who would not like to reach a target audience simply waiting to share your creative and engaging contents? - For businesses inclined to powerful visual contents, Tumblr is largely an untapped community, and of course, an unexplored opportunity.

Here are the following opportunities— mostly no-brainers, but just applying some common sense— for you to tap to promote your business on Tumblr:

🖥 Concentrate On Blogging With Great Images – **Photos predominate on Tumblr, crowding 78% of its posts. Besides, they are the most popular to share or re-blog.**

🖥 Link Your Tumblr Account to All Applicable Sites (i.e., website, weblog, Facebook (thru the Tumblelog app), and Instagram – **As it could apparently be difficult to convert sales or bag a lead from your Tumblr blog, ensure connecting your blog to your social media sites for more business engagement. This helps to double your exposures with only a little extra effort.**

🖥 Link Your Images/Videos To Your Tumblr Page – **Regardless of how viral are your website photos or videos, they always allow Tumblr users finding their way back to your business.**

🖥 Follow Other Tumblelogs – **Show your support to the Tumblr community and be a part of it by posting the blogs you follow.**

🖥 Install The Tumblr Social Sharing Button On Your Website – **To broaden your social media reach, urge your readership to repost or share your contents on multiple social media channels.**

💻 <u>Optimize Blogging By Using Hashtags</u> – Let a larger segment of your audience discover your contents on Tumblr by affixing hashtags to your posts.

💻 <u>Respond Quickly To Comments</u> – Engagement is king in social media. Reposting, linking, and commenting will increase engagement and earning the trust of your followers.

💻 <u>Limit The Playing Time Of Your Video Posts</u> – Always, keep your videos as short as possible. Videos with a playing time of less than a minute long usually receive 40% more engagement compared to videos playing from 10 to 20 minutes.

Your video's main intent should just be presenting a complete information package with call-to-action at the end. Moreover, click-through rates rise by 4% when posting videos with 15-second or less playing time as opposed to those 60-second or longer videos that only incur a 2% CTR.

💻 <u>Inject A Little Humor In Your Videos</u> – Page visits increase by 2% when visitors watch a funny video compared to ones that are more serious.

Truly, when combining blogging with social media, Tumblr can be a real force to reckon with. In fact, it continues to grow and remains among the world's top 30 websites with heavy traffic.

*"In this age of micro-blogging and two-second sound bites, almost no one has the attention span or time to read more than a few sentences."*

― **Tim Frick**

# Chapter 8 – Social Media Photo and Video Sharing Sites

*"We would not be distracted by comparison if we are captivated (by images and videos) with purpose."*

— **Bob Goff**

'A picture is worth a thousand words,' so goes the old cliché. Normally, we are fond of pictures. Adding a visual experience in a message transforms it quickly into a more personal relationship.

Thus, social media sharing sites enable their users to upload and post multimedia files like photos, audios, videos, and even slide presentations that are accessible from around the world. Thereafter, people will be able to share the uploaded contents with the rest of the world or simply, with a select circle of friends and associates.

**In addition, most of these social media sharing sites allow you to post your uploaded multimedia files on other social media outlets by embedding them. This is one reason why several marketers often use social media sharing sites apart from bringing practical or emotional values of sharing the message of their businesses with images or videos. Besides, it is generally quicker to create videos than writing an entire text.**

Typically, social media sharing sites receive huge amounts of traffic. Hence, these sites always become the ideal means to attract your leads and potential customers by getting your business involved and developing a large following.

In this book, it includes a couple of media types that marketers need to take into account. On one hand are those video sharing sites such as the famous YouTube and the durable Vimeo that can be convenient sites to post ads of products or services or tutorials for customer support. On the other hand, are those major photo-sharing sites that can be helpful to brands and are able to host videos like Pinterest, Instagram, and Flickr.

*Pinterest*

Pinterest operates as a free web and mobile application social media site with a software system created and aimed to discover a miscellany of niche information on the Web. It uses chiefly images on a smaller scale, videos, and GIFs.

The site summarizes itself as a *'catalog storage of ideas,'*

| | |
|---|---|
| **Founder(s)** | Paul Sciarra<br>Evan Sharp<br>Ben Silbermann |
| **Founded** | 21 March, 2006 |
| **Website** | www.pinterest.com |
| **Site Type** | Visual Discovery/<br>Collection/Storage |
| **Alexa Rank** | #67 (Apr. 2017) |
| **Users** | 200 million (Jan. 2018) |
| **Areas Served** | Worldwide |

*Image – 29: Pinterest Social Media Profile Information (2018)* inspiring its users to *'discover, go out of their shells, and embrace that concept,'* instead of posturing itself as an image-based social media platform. Pinterest users can upload, sort, save (previously termed as, 'Pin It'), and manage their selected images, termed as *'pins,'* and other media contents through categorized or themed collections, known as *'pinboards.'*

You can save pins from another user's pinboard, for which Pinterest termed it, *'repinning.'* You can also find contents for pinning outside of Pinterest, and upload them to your created pinboard using the 'Save' button. **You may download this button to your bookmark bar on your browser, or your webmaster can install it directly on your website to enable other Pinterest users to pin them right on your site.**

In 2013, Pinterest started displaying ads by way of *'promoted pins.'* Promoted pins are derivatives of a user's interests and activities on the platform or a consequence of visiting an advertiser's website.

During the same year, it also introduced the *'rich pin'* tool for enhancing the customer experience upon browsing through pins created by businesses. Two years later, Pinterest unveiled another convenient feature, which enabled users to search with images rather than words.

Its business pages include storing a wide array of various information and topics (previously termed as, 'interests'). Typically, these data involve prices of certain products, movie reviews and ratings, recipe ingredients, and fashion from head to toe.

Just recently, Pinterest had allowed businesses to create their own pages aimed at exposing and promoting their brands online. With such pages, the platform can well serve to be your virtual storefront. A case study in one fashion business website manifested that customers visiting from Pinterest have spent $180, which is more than half of the amount spent by customers coming from Facebook.

These customers have actually spent less time on the business' website, rather choosing to browse products from the business' pinboards. Further similar studies have persistently shown Pinterest to be more effective at creating sales than other social media sites. The Dublin-based digital marketing company, Wolfgang Digital, found in their study that website traffic coming from Pinterest business pages generated a relatively higher engagement by spending time on the business website for up to five times longer.

The latest feature implemented by Pinterest was, *'instant ideas,'* in 2017. This allows marketers to reach their consumers via the camera of their smartphones.

Pinterest is planning to add them eventually to the displayed results when users apply the *'lens'* feature for scanning an image from their phone to search for related images or pins. Alternatively, users can also apply the *'shop-the-look'* feature, which allows them to tap products featured in an image that will be revealing a listing of links to similar products that are available for purchase.

Pinterest Statistics Social Media Marketers Should Know:

The subsequent data are brief analyses of the different categories of current Pinterest users who comprise 31% of Internet users:

🖥 Industry/User Topics – Summarily, the pins on Pinterest are generally about food and beverages. This topic comprises about 20% of all pins. Crafts and home decor comes in second at 15%. Forming the rest of the 65% of the pins are, hobbies, fashion, pets, photography, miscellaneous products, etc.

🖥 Demographics – The bulk of Pinterest users are women, composing 81% of all users. Men can only manage 7% of all the comments recorded on the site. Out of all these users, 60% come from the U.S. while 32% are of Hispanic origins.

On a daily basis, the majority of its users are under 40 years old. Specifically, people falling under the 18 to 29 years old age group registers to be the most frequent users of the platform at 32%. People within the 65 years old and above age group are the least frequent users, tallying only 16%.

Of all the Pinterest users, high school graduates or with lesser educational background composes 25% while people with some college education or college graduates make up for 37%. The highest income group represents 30% while the lower income brackets consist 24%. However, more than 50% of all Pinterest users belong to the high socio-economic strata of the global society.

🖥 Geographical Location – Unbelievably, people living permanently in suburban areas account for 34% of Pinterest users. The urban permanent residents are neglectful to Pinterest, recording only 26%. The remaining 40% spreads across transient dwellers and constant travelers.

**List of Must-Have Pinterest Applications:**

With the rapid growth of mobile gadgets, more people are inclined consuming content or networking socially via handheld devices. Choosing any of the following Pinterest mobile apps should alter your social media experience on Pinterest towards updating yourself and profiting while on the go.

🖥 iPhone Smartphone and iPad Tablet – The iPhone, iPad and iPod Touch gadgets can apply all Pinterest functionalities under a single iPhone operating system (iOS).

🖥 Android Smartphone – Although this does not apply all the Pinterest functions as the iOS app does, it can at least pin your images, which is the most important Pinterest function of all.

🖥 Windows Smartphone – Currently, no standard Pinterest apps are available for phones with a Windows operating system (OS) except using a third-party Pinterest app, which is Scrapbook for Pinterest. This app functions well using a Windows Phone 7.5 or 8.0, but its only downside is that carries ads heavily and require subscription fees.

🖥 Pin4Ever – For a safe storage of your files, this app allows you to create a backup file for all your pins on your Android phone or any file storage device.

🖥 PinHog for Pinterest – This is a unique Pinterest app that allows you to be mobile, yet, minimize your extra data fees while you browse the Web for pins. The app not only enables you to browse while being offline but also, it provides you prerogatives of scheduling when you would want to pin files to your board.

🖥 PinPuff – This Pinterest monitoring tool tracks trends and lets you analyze the performance of your account. It can also calculate monetary values of your pins and determine what type of traffic these pins generate for you.

🖥 PinReach – Similar to PinPuff, the app provides you with data on how well you influenced others on the site. It also gives a Klout score, informing you about trends and your diminishing influence.

🖥 Reachli (previously, Pinerly) – With a user-friendly dashboard interface, the app continuously helps you find like-minded users, updates you on your pin schedule, or simply, unfollow groups.

🖥 Snapito – If your preference is surfing the Internet to take full-length web page screenshots to pin on your Pinterest page, then this free app can satisfy your needs.

🖥 Wisestamp – Although this may not be a Pinterest-specific app, it allows you to add a 'follow' button to your Pinterest account at the bottom portion of your emails that features all your latest pins.

**How to Market Your Business on Pinterest:**

Before marketing your products or service with the visual social media platform, you should first learn the Pinterest basics— creating your profile, creating pinboards, pinning images/videos, and following others. Think of the platform just as others do— a sort of a digital scrapbooking system with an array of wish list online. Feed your target market with images/videos of your brand that they want to see.

🖥 Explore And Learn the Trending and Latest Topics/Keywords– This will help you to determine what types of contents to pin. **For instance, when discovering a posting trend about DIY projects, then it calls for you to look for and share DIY contents that have potentials of relating back to your business.**

Users discover more about your brand whenever you are able to relate some trending topics back to your business. Alternatively, use trending keywords to decide on what type of contents you should create.

**When looking for relevant keywords, you just type in a keyword in the search bar and check out the suggested keywords flashed right under the search bar. You should try to include those suggested keywords in your contents' titles and descriptions.**

🖥 Implement Your Advertising Campaigns On Pinterest – Pinterest ads, or simply, promoted pins appear as regular pins on the site. The only difference is that you will be paying for your pins so people can see them.

About 73% of pinners declared that contents from brands augment the usefulness of Pinterest's services. In effect, 61% confirmed they were able to buy an item after viewing a business's content.

Apply geographic targeting with your ads so people in your specified location can see them. **Depending on the keywords and topic you used, advertising on Pinterest is affordable and produces a snowball effect.** Users will be seeing your ads and repin them, and thereby, your brand will be receiving extra exposures through repinning without shelling out for it.

💻 <u>Examine your Pinterest Analytics</u> – Pinterest Analytics, which you can find at the upper left corner of your profile page, informs you not only about who views your pins and page but also, the demographics of your audience, type of devices that visitors of your page use, and a list of your most popular pins.

Pinterest Analytics also provides you with data of averages of your profile page's daily impressions, monthly viewers, and monthly engagements. **A good understanding of your analytics data can help you to learn more about navigating and using Pinterest.**

💻 <u>Install the 'Pin It' Button to Your Weblog/Website</u> – This button allows Pinterest users to pin easily and directly your contents from your website to their own pinboards. **It makes it simpler for everybody to be sharing contents from your website.**

💻 <u>Squeeze Your Creative Juices To Produce Fun And Unique Contents</u> – You have a number of ways generate fun and unique contents while promoting your business or brand:

➢ **Generate pincodes for your physical store or business.** – Pincodes are typically similar to quick response (QR) codes. They are special codes, which you create and download by clicking on the three dots above your pinboard, to unlock your curated pinboards and profile page on Pinterest. After printing out the code and placing it in your store, users can enter the code thru their smartphones, with which to take them directly to your recommended pinboards on Pinterest.

➤ Create a new pinboard that serves as a gift guide. – **Do not just limit pinning your latest products to your pinboards.** For other special occasions, create a new pinboard that can serve as a gift guide featuring your products.

However, in order for this particular pinboard not to appear like one massive ad for your business, including also those pins from other brands. During the 2017 holiday season, Pinterest introduced the 'Secret Santa' feature, which let shoppers search for lists of personalized gift items and ideas purely based on the pinboards of their friends and families.

➤ Present giveaways. – When planning to hold a promotion or contest, pin the prize to your relevant pinboards.

➤ Create a reading list. – Save inspiring books or articles and other good reads that relate to your business in a separate pinboard. Your visitors may find them interesting to read. For article pins you are still about to read or post live on the site, you can create a secret board for them in your bookmarks folder so you would not lose or forget all about them.

🖥 Ensure Employing Rich Pins – Rich pins are special types of pins that enable you to have a smoother and more direct usage of the site. They include further information about the image, descriptions of the pinner, and a click-through link. Find out more about using and enabling these helpful rich pins on the developer's page of Pinterest. Pinterest has four types of rich pins you may use, as follows:

➤ App pins – are the latest addition to the family of rich pins that allows users to share or download apps right from the site.

➢ Article pins – allow users to see automatically the headline, author, and description of the article. In effect, these pins distinguish your articles from other contents in the site while making them more searchable.

➢ Product pins – facilitate easy and convenient shopping on Pinterest. They show users the updated price of your product in real time, where they can purchase your pinned product, and a direct link to your pinboard of products or product page.

➢ Recipe pins – show essential recipe information such as the required ingredients, preparation and cooking times, serving details, and nutritional values.

🖥 Join In And Create Group Boards – Group boards are collaborative boards owned by a user who adds others so they can contribute or share ideas. These boards are useful, especially when you plan on working on a certain project or holding a big event since many users normally follow group boards and more people can see your board and pin ideas.

## Instagram

Owned by Facebook, Instagram is a Web-based, free mobile and desktop application social media network service that allows its

| | |
|---|---|
| | Instagram |
| FOUNDER(S) | Kevin Systrom, Mike Krieger |
| FOUNDED | 06 October, 2010 |
| WEBSITE | www.instagram.com |
| SITE TYPE | Mobile Photo Hosting |
| ALEXA RANK | #17 (Jan. 2018) |
| ACTIVE USERS | 800 million (Jan. 2018) |
| AREAS SERVED | Worldwide |

*Image – 30: Instagram Social Media Profile Information (2018)*

users to share photos and videos, either privately or publicly to pre-approved followers.

Originally, Instagram launched its free mobile app only for the iOS operating system. It was only after two years that it accommodated a version for Android devices. During the same time, it followed introducing its services with a feature-limited website interface, including apps for Windows 10 for both mobile and desktop devices.

Its main usage enables registered users to upload to the site photos or videos and apply selected digital filters to their images. Users can also add locations by using geotags.

Furthermore, users can affix hashtags to their image posts or link up their images to other contents on Instagram that feature a similar theme or general topic. More importantly, users are able to connect their account to other social media networks, and thus, allowing them to share their images to those sites as well.

Initially, a unique feature of Instagram was the confinement of images to a rigid square frame; fortunately, it has now updated this feature and allowed users the liberty to post images in full size, whether in landscape or portrait size. Its *'Explore'* tab shows users a miscellany of media, which include curated contents, trending and popular photos and those taken at nearby locations, recommended video channels, and trending tags and locations.

Its support for videos has first allowed for a maximum of 15 seconds playing duration with limited quality. It was only recently that Instagram augmented their video support for longer and widescreen videos. It also has a private messaging system, termed as, 'Instagram Direct,' equipped with the basic photo-sharing functionality.

Its latest update is the introduction of the 'Stories' feature, which allows users to add images to share all the moments of their day, appearing together as a slideshow format. **Other new updates were the addition of virtual stickers and objects.**

The quick rise and popularity of Instagram led to a widespread community engagement. Users are deep into dedicated *'trends,'* wherein they post certain types of images on certain days of the week with a hashtag typifying a common theme. Fact is that Instagram keeps receiving positive reviews that it boasts itself as being one of the world's most influential social media network.

**Instagram Statistics Social Media Marketers Should Know:**

**Amongst rival social media networks, Instagram is an all-around powerhouse that marketers must consider.** At the rapid rate it grows, social media statisticians believe its MAU can reach a billion by the end of 2018. That is more than twice the MAU of Twitter and more than thrice as many users on Facebook Messenger and WhatsApp.

Ease of use and visual aesthetics are the twin aspects that truly make Instagram prosperous for marketers and essential for businesses. Apart from these major enticing aspects, the following statistics are what make Instagram click while letting you know how to target, engage, and promote your products effectively to your customers.

💻 Users Preference – About 71% of businesses the U.S. use the photo/video hosting site while 80% of all users follow a particular business on the site. Based on Instagram records, more than 120 million of its users visited a website, received directions, contacted a business, and messaged directly or emailed a business in the month of March 2017 alone. All these activities only denote a certain level of interest that you can actually consider all these users as leads.

💻 Advertising Growth – Per recent data released by the intelligence and social media analytics platform, Klear, Instagram showed 171,000 ads in Q4 2017 against the 134,000 ads released in Q2 of the same year. In other words, Instagram ads had grown drastically by 28% in just half a year. Definitely, no other time is better to promote your business with and participate in the platform but now.

Of all Instagram ads, 25% of them are single videos. Although the most common ads on Instagram are photo ads, video ads have now been gaining a lot of traction.

💻 Engagements With Posts – Whereas, an Instagram post allows a maximum of 30 hashtags, research suggests that 11 hashtags turn out to have the optimum results. Nevertheless, Instagram posts having at least a single hashtag generate 12.6% more engagements compared to those without. This gives rise to an estimated 70% of hashtags on Instagram speaking about brands. For a more tangible result, about 30% of Instagram users were able to purchase an item they first encountered on the platform.

Instagram continues to promote the usage of its geotagging feature that it is no longer surprising why posts, which include a specific location, receive 79% more engagement against those without. What is more surprising is the steady growth of Instagram videos, for which consumption has grown to 40%.

However, photo posts still create 36% more likes compared to videos. Yet again, you should not keep posting images featuring standalone products. Your photo posts should also highlight faces. Instagram photo posts featuring faces receive 38% more likes as opposed to those without.

Lest you are now going to modify your digital content marketing strategy of featuring your brand in each of your posts, never neglect the *'80/20 rule.'* This rule states that you should ensure an 80% concentration of your content towards enlightening, educating, and engaging your target audience, with only about 20% reserved for self-promotion or marketing your brand.

💻 Schedules of Traffic Volume and Advertising – Weekdays entail the most user engagements on Instagram. The safest days and time for posting with a maximum engagement are Tuesdays through Fridays, with Thursdays having the highest number of engagements between 9 A.M. to 6 P.M. Sundays incur the weakest engagement.

💻 Demographics – Instagram has a large international following, with 80% of its users living outside the U.S. Although the older age groups have begun gravitating towards the platform, 59% of the age group between 18 and 29 years old are the most frequent users of Instagram.

List of Must-Have Instagram Applications:

Marketing on Instagram has gone a long way from its beginnings when users only took photos and added a filter to the app.

Nowadays, you have entire apps dedicated only to either photo editing or graphic design, platform management or video creation! The following are the best-recommended apps you need for promoting your business on Instagram.

💻 Recommended Photo Editing Apps – Success on Instagram means you are able to post great and high-quality images. Thus, you will need any of these following powerful, yet, free photo-editing apps for iOS, Android, and web systems depending on your requirements:

➢ A Color Story – is your ideal app for specifically creating bright and colorful photos (available free for iOS).

➢ Snapseed by Google – is a free photo-editing app with powerful editing features (available free for both iOS and Android).

➢ VSCO Cam – as the most predominant branded hashtag on the site, the app helps you to sort through a wide variety of filters to add on your photos (available free for both iOS and Android).

➢ Layout by Instagram – is for displaying a collage that allows you to combine a maximum of nine photos into a single picture to post on the site (available free for both iOS and Android).

➢ Line Camera – is your ultimate app for capturing selfies! Although selfies are not applicable to all businesses, they could be useful for business bloggers and creatives for their personal brands (available for both iOS and Android).

➢ Foodie by Line Camera – is exclusively for food-related businesses for enhancing food photos (available free for both iOS and Android).

💻 Recommended Graphic Design Apps– You can communicate with your message better and quicker when you can add texts to your photo posts on Instagram. Graphic design apps will help you in this aspect without having to worry whether your followers have read your captions. Among these ideal and easy-to-use graphic design apps are the following:

➢ Canva for iPad – is originally the noted graphic design app for websites, but is now expanding its usage to the iPad app for creating images while you are on the go This app is especially useful when posting flyers for your upcoming business events, creating social media graphics, or just simply harnessing your collection of stock photos.

➢ Over – is your go-to app for creating social media images that could be shareable (available free for both iOS and Android).

➢ Quick by Over – is the perfect app for adding a slogan, tagline, or quote to your photo prior to its posting (available free for iOS).

💻 Recommended Apps for Managing Your Instagram Account – Benchmark your marketing efforts on Instagram by using these apps for helping you to monitor your performance and success, schedule your postings, and shop on your feed.

➢ LIKEtoKNOW.it — is for bloggers who would like to earn commissions from their followers who shop at their Instagram looks. Procedurally, bloggers post a URL in the caption of their Instagram photo. Once their followers 'liked' the photo, they will be receiving an email containing links to shop their look (refer to Image-31).

*Image –31: Illustrative Procedures for Using the LIKEtoKNOW.it App on Instagram*

At present, it is only available to bloggers within the reward Style network— a Dallas-based company that operates a monetization platform for lifestyle, beauty, and fashion influencers (available free for the web app).

➢ Later (previously, Latergramme) – saves you precious time with your marketing activities on Instagram by helping you to collaborate with your team members, preview your Instagram feed, and schedule your posts across multiple Instagram accounts. Since auto-posting can get your Instagram account banned, the app sends a push notification on your phone when it is high time for you to post (available free for iOS).

➢ Iconosquare – sets up your Instagram analytics dashboard to monitor your engagement performances and the growth of your followers, as well as informing you for the most popular times to post on the site (available free for the web app).

💻 Recommended Apps for Video Creations – If you like to create a short video for your Instagram feed, then the following video creation apps will help you to edit your short videos using your phone, wherever you may be:

➢ YouTube Capture – is an easy-to-use app exclusively created for YouTube, but it can still function well for Instagram by helping you to stabilize your videos while you are recording them. You can add music or audio elements to your video and multiple clips together, as well as trimming these clips (available free for iOS).

➢ Hyperlapse by Instagram – allows you to create easily time-lapse videos using your phone. Time-lapse videos involve a series of still shots captured over a certain period, and after which, woven together and fast-tracked them as a video. You will have choices for your preferred video speed. The app has a built-in image stabilization, implying that you need not have to worry about retaining your hands in a still position while taking the video (available free for iOS).

➢ iMovie – is the mobile app version of the Mac app for video creations. It has more advanced controls such as the addition of filters and video enhancement effects like fast forward playing, split screen, and slow motion (available free for iOS).

**How to Promote Your Business on Instagram:**

Whether your marketing campaign strategy requires updating or you are yet a newbie to social media marketing or social media networking, you will surely find these following tips on how to apply and master Instagram for your business satisfactorily useful:

💻 **Exhibit Your Creativity On The Platform** – Do not hide what you do; show it in a more creative way. Concentrate on solutions you offer, and never about the goods you sell.

It is important on Instagram when you add value to your target audience and look good while you do your way. Always think about and put a premium on visual content, which is your most significant asset (and failure) on Instagram.

If you have a service-oriented business, then focus on highlighting the operations behind offering your services. Exhibit the culture of your business; inform the world about your mission; or, you can simply share valuable tips and guidelines. You can show all of these by uploading and posting photos, short videos (akin to GIFs, known as, Boomerangs) and videos with up to a minute in length.

Take advantage of 'Instagram Stories.' Adverts or promotions thru Instagram Stories can help you to target new sets of audiences and include a call-to-action to your collages. Although the Instagram Story is only on the mobile app, you can send it as a direct message.

💻 **Build A Winning Profile** — Your Instagram profile is the anchor of your presence on the channel. It creates the first impressions of your brand. Furthermore, your profile is the only window where you are able to provide a link anywhere on the site.

Also in your profile is your bio description, which provides you with a limited 150-character of prime space to show to your visitors who you are, what you do, your website, what you are offering, and why your visitors should care. Note that Instagram is the king of social media engagement and you should draw an accurate and engaging picture of your brand, product, or service on the site. **Hence, it is worth investing your time to get your profile right at the very start.**

💻 **Show Customers Behind-The-Scenes Videos Of The Making Of Your Product** — Generally, customers have the tendency of being curious about where products come from or how businesses produce them. Thru Instagram, you can show to people the entire lifecycle of your product, especially when your business promotes Fair Trade-certified or environmentally friendly products. Source your images to illustrate how you produce your products — from their raw materials, production, packaging, and distribution.

💻 **Expand Your Target Audience By Using Hashtags** — The use of hashtags on any social media site can truly expand your reach. Hashtags are an ideal way to facilitate users to search for contents related to your business and website, as well as your principal Instagram account. **Your hashtags may be generic or campaign-specific. What is of import is their relevance. Ensure also setting up your chief business hashtag (i.e., #yourbrandname). However, use your hashtags sparingly over Instagram to avoid annoying your customers.**

💻 <u>Cite And Collaborate With Others</u> – Work with others on the site and mention them (i.e., @nameofcollaborator). For this reason, you simply want others to notice your business or presence on the site. For all you know, Instagram is one of the leading and most potent social media outlets for highlighting partners or collaborators and sharing success stories of customers.

Although you do not collaborate officially with a non-profit group, you can promote a fundraiser or give to charity, perhaps, twice a year. This is beneficial for as long as their causes reflect your company's mission and values of your brand.

Note that not all users are tracking hashtags on social media. Therefore, tagging or citing an account is typically a more prudent choice for getting your business or presence on Instagram noticed well.

*You can also apply another tactic, which involves using a 'shout-out'. On one hand, an unpaid shout-out is collaborating with another particular brand, which has approximately a similar follower count as you do, to promote each other's business to your corresponding audiences. Both of you can benefit from this activity thru increased exposure.*

On the other hand, a paid shout-out usually entails a bigger budget since it is essentially a campaign using the services of an influencer (i.e., brand or celebrity, who both have a larger following). However, for as long as the audience of the influencer is genuine and you are able to create a strong call-to-action on your campaign, then a paid shout-out is a useful technique to gain quickly massive new sets of followers.

💻 <u>Keep Your Customers Anticipating And Offer Them Exclusivities</u> – An important part of effective social media marketing is to keep your customers interested. For your loyal fans and followers, reward them with exclusive contents. Enable them to be the primary people to know and learn about your new products, services, or business events (i.e., conferences, webinars, sales promotions, etc.).

*You can also create teaser photos that can build within them the element of anticipation or the curious satisfaction for your latest product releases, launches, and office or store openings. These typical previews let your followers feel special and important, and more importantly, compel them to keep coming back and learn more insider information.*

💻 <u>Analyze Your Instagram Performance And Work Upon It</u> – If you will never take a step back and make a review of your marketing efforts— what have worked and did not— your social media marketing strategy remains a guessing game. Fact is that you can digest all the helpful articles in the world about social media marketing and its best practices, but in the end, you will only figure out what truly works best for your customers through measuring and testing results.

You can always access easily from a wide selection of the various social media management and measuring tools (i.e., Klout, PeerIndex, etc.) to help you through this aspect. Use them not only to schedule in advance your campaigns but also, to measure how they successfully ran. Ensure to measure regularly your engagement, clicks, and follower count so you can fine tune and improve your strategy.

*YouTube*

| YouTube | |
|---|---|
| FOUNDER | Steve Chen<br>Chad Hurley<br>Jawed Karim |
| FOUNDED | 14 February, 2005 |
| WEBSITE | www.youtube.com |
| SITE TYPE | Video Hosting |
| ALEXA RANK | #2 (Oct. 2017) |
| ACTIVE USERS | 1.5 billion (Jan. 2018) |
| AREAS SERVED | Worldwide (except blocked countries) |

*Image – 32: YouTube Social Media Profile Information (2018)* media sharing platforms. Generally, these sites allow their registered members to upload videos, usually free, for which anyone can view them on their site or watch their embedded versions on a certain website or weblog.

Most of these sites offer users sharing options, either private or public and almost similar services. Nevertheless, the most popular video-sharing site of all is YouTube, based on the latest rankings conducted by the noted web-traffic analysis outfit, Alexa.

YouTube enables users to view, upload, comment, rate, add to favorites, share, and report on videos, as well as subscribing to other user channels. The site offers a massive and broad selection of corporate media or user-generated videos. Available contents range from video and TV show clips to movie trailers, from documentary and short films to live streams, and from audio recordings to music videos. Additionally, it accommodates other contents like original and personal short videos, video blog (also known as a vlog), and educational or tutorial videos.

Individuals upload most of the materials on YouTube; however, big media outfits such as the BBC, CBS, Hulu, and Vevo (short for video evolution, which is also a video hosting site) offer some of their contents via YouTube, being part of the partnership program provided by YouTube. As of present, more than a million members are with YouTube's Partnership Program.

*Actually, YouTube earns ad revenues from Google AdSense, which is a program targeting ads corresponding to the type of audience and site content. YouTube's vast majority of their videos are free to watch, except film rentals, subscription-based premium channels, and 'YouTube Red'— a video subscription* service that offers ad-free access to YouTube, including access to more exclusive contents created in partnership with its users.

A huge portion of the revenues goes to the video's copyright holders. When YouTube first launched in 2007 its Partnership Program— a system derived on AdSense that allows the video uploader to share the revenues generated by advertising on the platform— YouTube normally takes a 45%-share of the ad revenues from videos in the program, while 55% goes to the uploader.

**Nonetheless, as of the latest update on January 16, 2018, YouTube made drastic changes on the eligibility requirements for monetization within the partnership program. A user's channel only becomes eligible to the program if it has at least a thousand subscribers and reached a minimum of 4,000 hours of viewing time over the past 12 months.** Although this declaration affected many, YouTube only wants to ensure that uploaded videos for monetization would never involve any controversy (i.e., a breach of intellectual property rights, copyright infringements, etc.).

Apparently, the update somehow penalized smaller user channels. For this reason, it continues to stir criticisms from the public. However, YouTube recognizes the virtue of fair play through its Play Buttons— an essential component of the YouTube Creator Rewards— that offers deserving recognition (by way of trophies) to the most popular channels on YouTube.

YouTube Statistics Social Media Marketers Should Know:

By hosting more than a billion users all over the world, YouTube statistics are as enormous as its number of users. However, here is just a list of the most important ones that could help guide your campaign on the site:

🖳 Usage and Preference – YouTube has seen a great user growth by more than 60% since 2013. Daily usage of the site has even increased by more than 40% year-after-year. Hence, its video traffic tallies over five billion a day, apart from the daily uploading of more than 300 hours of video playing time per minute and the daily downloading of about ten million videos.

🖳 Demographics – The main traffic of YouTube mostly come from the 18 to 49 years old age bracket. On one hand, males comprise only 44% of its users, and mostly watch sports and other online game-related videos.

On the other hand, women aged between 13 and 27 years old comprise 17.5% of the 56% female users on the site. The female-dominated video categories on YouTube are the most enticing for particular businesses. These categories are mostly involving brands, products, or services, for which certain marketers promote (refer to Image-33).

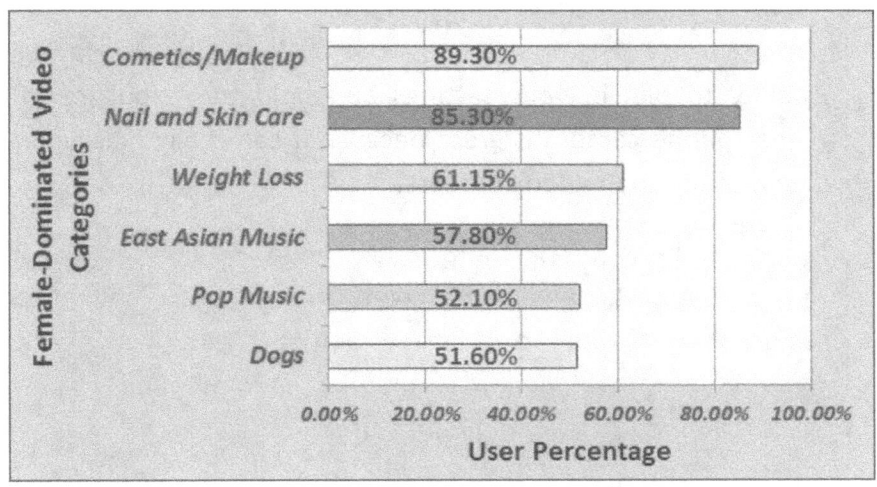

Image – 33: Percentage of Female Viewership over Their Dominated Video Categories

On a monthly basis, the U.S. has the most YouTube users with 168 million, followed by Brazil with 70 million, and Russia with 48 million. Outside the U.S., YouTube views have risen by more than 80%.

**List of Must-Have YouTube Applications:**

Most apps marketers implement when using YouTube are those having photo/video enhancing abilities. For, after all, you have nothing to upload to the site but photos and videos. Here are the most basic free apps that include video management on the site:

💻 Snapseed – is a photo-editing app, which you would use for your thumbnails inside your videos. It allows you to add color brightness, contrast, saturation, and ambiance to your photos and all other aspects to make your photos grab viewers' attention and stand out from the other thumbnail photos on You Tube's video list. You can actually edit your photos while you are on the go (available free for iOS, Android, and Chrome web app).

💻 Open Camera for Android Smartphones – lets you dial in all your settings for your smartphone camera. It has all the adjustments that make your photos look better. Having that ability to dial in your settings and hold the exposure in your smartphone camera is great because it can really help you shoot beautifully your video contents.

💻 Legend – is the best app to use when you like to add texts to your videos. It can convert texts into amazing animations. In short, it turns your words into motion to inspire people and make your subscribers laugh, sympathize, guided, and enjoy your uploaded videos. **You only have to put in your texts and the app will pre-make all these awesome graphics into text slides in between sections of your videos.**

💻 YouTube Studio Creator – lets you organize your YouTube channel, manage your uploaded videos, and interact with your subscribers. **The app has several tools namely, Dashboard, Video Manager, Community, Channel, Analytics, and Audio to help you to perform all these tasks.**

💻 Google Keep – is a note-taking app that helps you organize your thoughts and ideas with anything that you wish to do on your YouTube channel or website. **The app can capture quickly your present thoughts and share them with your subscribers. It can also transcribe automatically what you speak in a voice memo while you are on the go.**

Additionally, you can add to the app all your important notes or lists and photos (i.e., receipt, documents, posters, etc.) lest forgetting them. You can organize easily or find them later in Google Keep Search.

### How to Market Your Business on YouTube:

**When you are searching for ways to receive word regarding the products or services that your business promotes,** you should never ignore YouTube as one of your best marketing tools. Its massive audience and multimedia formatting offer a greatly effective way of communicating your brand message to your target audience. Besides, your business can market on the platform with a relatively low cost. The following are your guide to gain the attention and interest of your audience from uploading your videos to YouTube:

💻 **Communicate Personally with Your Customers** – **An old adage in the marketing business says, 'You just really have to sell yourself.' In short, people simply want to purchase goods from people or businesses they have known and trusted.**

**YouTube offers your business a superb medium to present your brand and yourself while letting your target audience feel as if they know you.** Upload one or multiple videos to the site that would introduce your business or yourself, and discuss what you offer and why your business exists.

You must let your target customers feel comfortable in your introduction. Show to them that you truly care about helping them to satisfy their special requirements, solve their problems, and care about their personal experiences with your brand.

Keep these videos short, perhaps, a minute of playing time at the most. Take note that your objective is to let your leads make a fast and positive impression of your brand. Never bore them with unnecessarily excessive details.

💻 **Highlight The Best Features Of Your Products** – Upload multiple and unique videos that show off to your target audience your product from different close-up angles. In these videos, let them know why your product is of high quality, reliable, and easy to use.

Hence, you can upload videos of your products while in use, which will highlight the capabilities of your product and make your audience think about how they could apply your product to satisfy their needs. This translates abstract benefits into tangible and feasible solutions in the minds of your audience.

💻 Manifest Your Own Expertise – **Having and showing the bragging rights about your expertise and authority never makes an impression.** Your only way to make your business expertise to keep on shining through is uploading informative videos that contain tips and pointers, results of conducted product tests and studies, case histories that demonstrate provided solutions, and other pertinent materials that describe your business expertise and make them all believable to your target audience. If you cannot make a good video out of all these, then you can always create and annotate a brief PowerPoint presentation.

💻 Present Testimonials From Other Customers – **Your customers generally identify themselves with other customers.** Hence, when you are having customers raving about your brand, never hesitate and be afraid to have their permission of taking videos about relating their real experiences with your product. **Whether your customers were pleased particularly with you, your brand, or both, their messages will always turn into a potent voice in favor of you and your business.** Let them be the real and willing ambassadors of your brand.

However, never encourage these customers to present your video testimonials in your corporate office or a recording studio. You just ask them simply if you could record their comments with your smartphone. Videos appear more believable than they would if you record them midst an informal setup; along the process, you can gain more enthusiasm from your viewers.

When your raving customer speaks to you over the phone and has access to an internet connection, encourage them to join you in a session of Google+ Hangouts on Air. Ask their permission to get a video recording of the hangout and its uploading to YouTube.

💻 <u>Offer In-Depth Instructional Videos Associated With Your Brand</u> – Regardless if your product is complicated to use or not, post tutorial videos that will demonstrate a systematic guide to the proper applications of your product. From a marketing perspective, doing so makes more sense than never doing it at all since your customers often want to learn and understand what truly involves when using a product prior to buying it.

For example, when you are demonstrating a software application product, you can show in your videos how to get it started, and thereafter, how to apply each feature of the software. These uploaded instructional videos shall be in association with your engaged or call-to-action videos, pleasant messages to your customers, and testimonials in order for your customers to get a good grasp of your business and product.

A study stated that the ideal playing time of these typical videos should be within 5 minutes or less. You might want to cover these videos separately (i.e., assembling the product, operational steps, safety tips, using the special features or accessories, etc.).

More often than not, potential customers prefer more to view such videos than reading a manual. Besides, these how-to videos provide you added benefits you since they result in the reduction of support calls.

💻 <u>Perform Real-Time Marketing</u> – Consider to host video events live (i.e., new product launch, replies to customers' FAQ, interview with authorities on topics related to your industry, workshops, and webinars) to give your business a more personal touch. **With a limited budget, you can perform this task thru scheduling a session in Google+ Hangouts on Air.**

Ensure to promote your promotional videos as soon as you uploaded them to the site. With approximately more than 300 hours of video that YouTube users upload for each minute, promoting your videos will help to get them found and viewed. Advertise the links to your videos on your email list, website, and posts to your other social media profiles.

## *Vimeo*

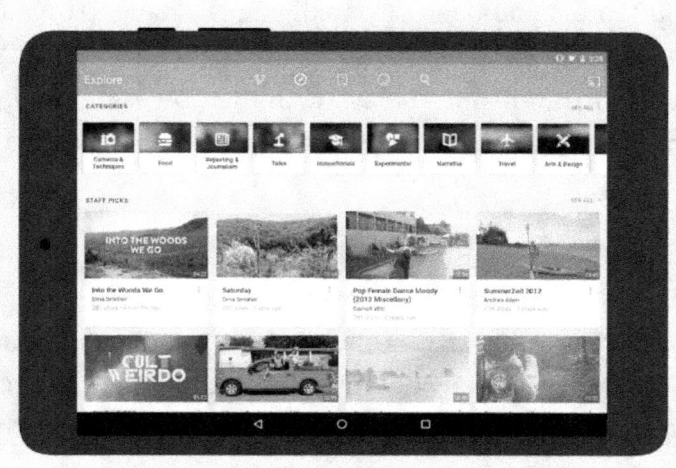

Vimeo is the first video hosting and sharing social media site that supported high-definition videos. The site concentrates more on short movies and films marketed under the *'Vimeo on Demand'* program.

| | |
|---|---|
| FOUNDER(S) | Zach Klein, Jake Lodwick |
| FOUNDED | November, 2004 |
| WEBSITE | www.vimeo.com |
| SITE TYPE | Video Hosting |
| ALEXA RANK | #135 (Nov. 2017) |
| ACTIVE USERS | 240 million (Jan. 2018) |
| AREAS SERVED | Worldwide |

*Image – 34: Vimeo Social Media Profile Information (2018)*

The program is an open platform enabling site members to sell their broadcast-quality work directly to the site's wildly passionate audience. When you are a Vimeo Business member ($600 total annual fee plus tax), you will have 5TB/year for storing HD videos, worldwide distribution of your videos as per your preferences, unlimited plays with the powerful capabilities of the Vimeo HD player, priority conversions, and access to more easy-to-use tools.

Vimeo Business also supports team collaboration, whereby, you can add up to ten team members to manage your videos and collaborate on private projects within your account. It further has an array of various video-marketing tools that capture emails to generate leads, link viewers from your videos with cards and publish videos as organic social posts.

The creation of Vimeo is actually a play on the words, 'video' and 'me,' and an anagram for 'movie'. Its core community of users comprises videographers, indie filmmakers, documentarians, and their followers. This community adopts the title, **'Vimeans,'** denoting a member of the Vimeo community who has regularly engaged actively with fellow users.

Vimeo registered users can upload, share, and watch videos with high-definition playback in 1280 × 720 (pixels). The site converts automatically your uploaded HD videos into 720/30p (video frame rate) VP6 flash video (video codec-formatted file type). Originally, the site re-encodes uploaded videos; but now, it encodes all the videos even into H.264 (or MPEG-4 AVC or advanced video coding) to support HTML5 programs.

In 2014, Vimeo launched its support of '4K Ultra-High Definition (UHD) image displays.' This includes the live-streaming of 4K contents, which offer four times the capabilities of showing razor-sharp and vivid video images with more light, depth, and shadow details compared to standard HD 1080p.

In 2017, the site introduced its support of 360-degree videos, which include supports for smartphones and virtual reality channels, stereoscopic videos, and the series of online videos that offer the 360-degree filming and production guidance. As such, Vimeo boosted its technology and acquired, in the same year, the Livestream services to become also a live-streaming platform.

***These technological innovations for the site's video contents benchmarked the criteria of its prime video selections from 'Staff Picks.' Staff Picks is a group composed of real human beings who work at Vimeo and handpick recommended videos for viewing.***

Vimeo Statistics Social Media Marketers Should Know:

Although YouTube is the undisputed leader in the video-sharing niche, Vimeo keeps on proving all these years as a formidable competitor. While the site does not boast of a billion users, it has, nonetheless, impressive usage statistics. Here are the following important numbers and facts that could help you in your campaigns on Vimeo:

💻 Usage and Preferences – The number of monthly viewers on the site has now reached over 240 million, or an average of 8 million viewers per day. These viewers accounted 715 million videos viewed per month or an average of close to 25 videos seen per user per day.

In relation to business users, North American B2B marketers comprise 20% of the users who distribute content. Still, 70% of all its users are living outside of the U.S., with 30 million in Africa and the Middle East, while 5 million are in Asia and the Pacific.

The percentage of users with high school qualifications or less is a measly 1.2%. Hence, the site denotes having a massive fan base of highly educated users. As proof of the platform's leadership in broadcast-quality and high-resolution contents, the number of subscribers— also called 'creators'— to Vimeo's myriad array of video enhancing tools and apps keeps on increasing and now tallies at over 800,000 users.

🖥 <u>Traffic Sources</u> – Majority of the traffic source of Vimeo comes from Search at close to 33.5%, while approximately 20% originate from the various social media networks (refer to Image-35). Facebook users usually visit the site with 59.3% of its users becoming Vimeo regulars.

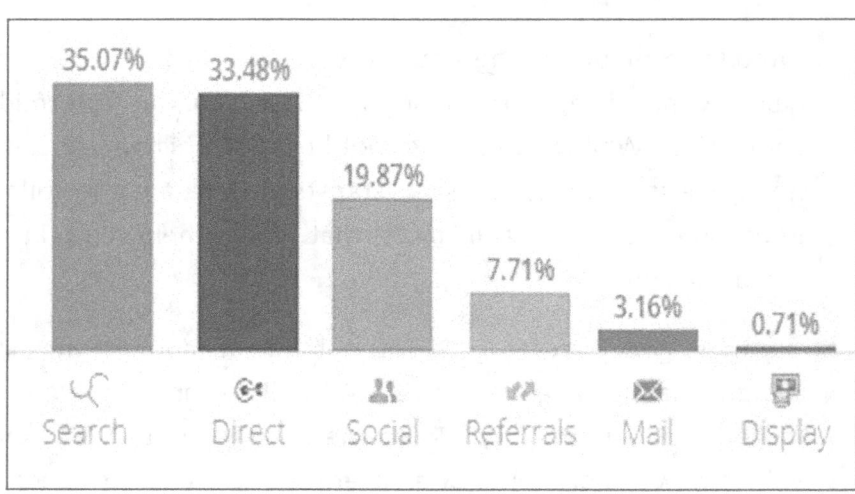

*Image – 35: Traffic Source Analyses on Vimeo (as of Feb. 2018)*

Traffic from referrals generally comes from the world's leading software development platform, github.com, which accounted for 3.5%. Display ads have the least traffic, with YouTube as the top publisher referring ad traffic to Vimeo.

🖥 <u>Viewed Categories</u> – Vimeo have 15 main video categories, namely: Food, Cameras & Techniques, Reporting & Journalism, Personal, Talks, Arts & Design, Fashion, Instructional, Experimental, Narrative, Music, Animation, Comedy, Travel, and Documentary. However, the interests of Vimeo audience are mostly inclined to other sub-categories, in order: Arts & Entertainment, Computer & Electronics or Software, News & Media, and Adult.

🖥 <u>User Engagement</u> – As of the latest period of Feb-Mar 18, 2018, Vimeo's total monthly visits dropped by 5% at 203.4 million from 214 million during the period of Jan-Feb 18, 2018. The average duration of each visit is a quick 3 seconds while visiting 3.36 pages. Overall, Vimeo has a relatively high bounce rate (percentage of visitors navigating away from the platform after viewing only a single page) of 60.2%.

**List of Must-Have Vimeo Applications:**

If you begin uploading your videos to Vimeo, you need not have too many applications to use since you and your audience can already truly enjoy the site's 4K Ultra-HD with high-dynamic range (HDR) imaging video enhancing and management tools. However, if you are to upload your videos while on the go, you may find it useful to use the following mobile apps, made especially for Vimeo:

- 💻 [Vimeo 2.0 for Android](#) – Built for your Android smartphone or tablet, the app can let you upload videos anywhere, anytime, as it transcodes them with gorgeous HD playback. It also allows you to explore curated categories suggested by the human-powered curation team, Staff Picks. You can also perform with the app those usual Vimeo tasks such as following creators and channels and watch as many videos you like.

- 💻 [Vimeo 6.0 for iOS](#) – You can experience the awesome power behind this app like the Android app plus its capability of playing away videos without a Wi-Fi connection. The app can save your selected videos for watching them offline (or deleting them from your playlist) when you are high up in the skies or deep under the ground. It also has integrated video editing tools to augment the enhancement of your videos (i.e., Cameo, Clips, Vidlab, FilmoraGo, Animoto, Splice, Quick, and iMovie).

## How to Market Your Business on Vimeo:

Vimeo offers no ads before, during, or after playing your videos. Hence, to truly expand and promote your business while creating customer loyalty on the site, you should offer value even prior to making a sales purchase.

An ideal way to retain your customers and acquire new ones is informing and teaching them how to perform better at what they are actually trying to do. Tutorial or instructional videos are effective methods to implement teaching to your potential leads and customers what you know and link up with them at each stage of the purchasing cycle.

💻 Think Creatively. Teach a Universal Skill — **When you teach difficult skills (e.g. computer programming or video editing), it usually requires some special expertise, which your business may not really have in-house. Nevertheless, that does not indicate your business has longer anything to teach your potential leads and customers.**

Think creatively about certain a subject or theme that anybody can build a practical advice on it. Everyone wants to learn some lessons, regardless of whomever one is or what you strive to sell them. Lessons resonating towards a wider scope of people are more likely to go viral or shared.

💻 Ask For Assistance — To broaden your base of expertise and authority, teach with a knowledgeable collaborator. This will help you to give more value to your target audience viewing your tutorial. You might also want to ask your collaborators to help you in terms of promoting your videos to their own social media networks.

💻 Coordinate or Connect Your Product with an Effective Relation — The best way to promote your brand or product is by demonstrating it in real action thru your videos. These videos must also include teaching your target customers some precious life skill. For instance, if you are in a tie business, you may want to show your sets of ties in a video that would include a tutorial or demo on how to tie a bowtie.

💻 Present New Perspectives — No matter what style you use in your tutorials or the topic you are teaching, ensure trying to create something innovative or unique, and connect it directly to your brand or product.

🖥 Give Away Your Secrets – **Never be afraid to reveal your secret tactics and teach your target customers how to perform what you perform best. For each individual who is willing to exhaust several hours doing-it-themselves, many more are very much willing to purchase the end-product upon coming to realize how difficult it is for them to do it themselves.**

🖥 Boost The SEO Value Of Your Videos – **Videos are worth a zillion words. Bolster up the SEO value of your instructional videos by optimizing their title and description. Use words you think people would be searching for to find your video tutorials. Transcribing your entire videos may also augment your SERP ranking.**

# Flickr

*Image – 36: Flickr Social Media Profile Information (2018)*

Flickr is a photo/video-hosting and sharing social media site and web services platform. Social media analysts tag the site as the best online photo- management and sharing social media app in the world. For this reason, Flickr has two principal objectives for its existence:

Firstly, Flickr wants to help you create your photos and make them available to other people who matter most to you. Whatever you may wish, especially promoting your business thru photos and videos on the site, Flickr helps you to make all these wishes possible, and with more!

To implement all these, Flickr gets photos and videos in and out of its system in as several different ways as possible, by scouring them from mobile devices, the Web, home computers of users, and whatever software people use in managing their content. The site also only wants to push all these pictures and videos in as many ways as it can— on the main Flickr platform, by email, in RSS feeds, or by posting to external blogs.

Secondly, Flickr aims to enable its users to organize their photos and videos in more innovative ways. As soon as people made the switch to digital, the volumes of photos they can capture or videos they shoot with their trigger-happy finger easily overwhelm them. Albums, which were the main systematic way for people to organize their photos and videos, are superb until accumulating 50 or more of them. While albums have lived up long to their basic functions, Flickr seems to be retiring them.

As a better resolve, Flickr wants to make a collaborative system for organizing all your photos or videos on the site. On one hand, the site has collaborated with Blurb— a self-publishing suite that allows its users to create, self-publish, share, promote, and sell their own eBooks and printed 'albums.' Blurb has all the available book production tools that can cater to people with various distinctive digital skills.

With Blurb, you can connect your Flickr account to its site and start creating your book. As for the layout of your book, you can import your Albums and Photostream (all the photos you uploaded, in the reverse order). After creating your book, you will have an array of options for customization and printing. These choices include a wide variety of paper options, creative captions and texts, numerous photo layouts, print-on-demand, offset printing, and other digital outputs.

You can then sell your printed project by selecting from a roster of distribution selections, which include Ingram, Amazon, and the Blurb Bookstore. When registered as a Flickr Pro, you have the bright opportunity of promoting your books on Flickr.

On the other hand, Flickr allows you also to give all your other contacts the permission to organize all your stuff on the site. Not only does it allow them to add comments but also, your contacts can add notes and tags. Since all these data grow together as metadata, they become also searchable, and thus, you will be able to find certain items much easier.

For bloggers, photographers, and even marketers or just about anybody who has a camera, Flickr has become a helpful and reliable photo/video-sharing services channel. The outlet, owned by Yahoo, and known for its convenient applications, has now an awesome collection of Creative Commons-licensed images, which assist publishers to search for royalty-free images.

Flickr keeps on evolving in so many ways. The design of its evolution is always to make everything easier and better for its users. You can check out your Flickr Blog to keep yourself updated about the site's latest developments.

**Flickr Statistics Social Media Marketers Should Know:**

Flickr statistics are not too many since the platform itself has the 'Statistics' section on a user's profile dashboard. Meaning, Flickr users can access easily the figures and other platform analytics data they need about their posts (i.e., number of recent and top views, as well as the breakdown of these views).

With Flickr Statistics, and along your various processes of using the platform, you will be able to gain an understanding of how other users are discovering your photos and videos on Flickr. You will also be able to see which of your posts are trending currently, and which among them were able to perform best over your entire course of using your Flickr account. However, a pair of significant statistics will indicate how useful the site is for your campaign strategies:

**First, Flickr receives monthly more than 7 billion application programming interface (API) requests. API is a set of protocols, sub-routine definitions, and tools for creating software and applications.** These requests denote that several users usually ask to get valuable information from Flickr's database (e.g., getting a list of all Flickr users from its database). That is actually procuring and having a ready email list of your target customers.

**Second, Flickr users upload an average of 25 million photos on any given high-traffic day.** This huge figure translates to an average of

1 million photos shared on the platform per day. By this hectic photo/video-sharing activity, this gives you the idea that you should always try to create shareable images, which also relate to your brand or product.

**List of Must-Have Flickr Applications:**

Since the site is a great tool for organizing your photos/videos and sharing them with the world, Flickr offers 1,000GB or 1TB of free space to store or backup your photos. **Yet, your experience on the platform can even be much better with the following useful third-party apps and tools that can facilitate managing your images and videos, uploading them faster, and helping you to discover new sets of interesting individuals to follow:**

💻 Juploadr – is a JavaScript-based cross-platform uploading app to get easily your photos off from the hard drive of your desktop/laptop and up to Flickr. **Although this tool is quite outdated, it still functions reliably and makes it more convenient for you to upload your photos in batches, while at the same time, keeping them organized.**

💻 Preloadr – is an image-editing tool that you can connect to your Flickr account. Using the app, you can select images you have uploaded previously, crop, rotate or flip, apply filters, and resize them. Additionally, you can see tags added automatically by your uploading app or camera.

💻 Lurvely – is an image-searching app that helps you to find beautiful imageries on Flickr. By default, you will be able to find images from the 'Interesting' stream section of the site, or those snapshots popular with the site's users. **It can actually be difficult** to find great and interest-based images on Flickr unless you join certain groups and photo pools. Hence, if you use this app, Lurvely converts into a portal where it shows you only the photos you have liked or favorited and give you more suggestions of great photos or photographers based on those you have already liked.

🖥 Retrievr – is also an image-searching app that enables you to find images by drawing simply a rough sketch of them in an appropriated box. This is more fun than functional; yet, if your fingers have that artistic touch, then you might just be able to find exactly the typical image you are looking for.

🖥 Flickr Commons Map – presents the latest uploaded photos for any geographic area displayed on the 'World Map'. You just zoom in on a definite portion of the world that interests you, and you will be able to see the number of photos available from that specific location and view them on Flickr.

**How to Market Your Business on Flickr:**

While perceptions arise that Flickr is in collusion with Yahoo, a well-built Flickr profile used creatively for business marketing and optimized for the search engines will help your brand positively. Hence, as a marketer, you should not ignore Flickr. When you use Flickr only for your personal photo albums online, you are actually in an ideal haven to expand your goals, especially when having a small business of your own. Flickr can promote your business visually. Here are a few tips to realize your added objectives:

🖥 Scour Stock Photography Requirements – Flickr is a great and rich source for stock photography requirements for your weblog. Alternatively, you can also provide your own stock photos to others so you can build relationships and goodwill with them while establishing brand recognition among them. **Regardless of whatever topic you write, various imageries are always available on Flickr to go with your article.** You can use the Flickr Photodropper, a WordPress plug-in that lets you search and import certain images from Flickr photos.

🖥 Take Advantage of Using Keywords – Since each uploaded image to Flickr lets you write its title, description, and keyword tags, take this opportunity to optimize your photos for SEO by being creative about your keywords. **Create the proper tags that can easily make people notice your brand or product.** Additionally, when writing about its description, try to include links to your website, weblog, or your other social media accounts so more people can find you.

> *"Social media is the ultimate equalizer as it changes our ways of communicating and how others perceive us, both positively and negatively. It gives a voice and a platform to anyone willing to engage. For each time you update your status or post a photo/video, you actually contribute to your own personal brand and digital footprints."*
>
> — **Amy Jo Martin**

# Chapter 9 – BONUS. Creating the Essential Elements of Your Ideal and Systematic Social Media Marketing Plan

*"Random social media tactics lead to random results. You need a strategy."*

— **Stephanie Sammons**

After having an overview of all the pertinent social media sites for promoting your business, you might seem to need extra assistance for jumpstarting your social media campaign strategy. Foremost, you may wonder what would be the basic, yet, most significant factors to include in your campaign.

**Actually, your business goals and purposes will be your guiding light to your campaign strategy so you can connect successfully connect with your leads and target customers. However, before you can start, try to review some important basics.**

**Your social media marketing plan will be the summary of about everything you are planning to do and wish to achieve for your brand or business by using the previously discussed social media networks. This plan must comprise a general audit about where your social media accounts stand at present; the goal of leading your business to where you want it to be in the future; and, all the necessary apps and tools you should use to get there.**

Thus, if you are more specific with your campaign plan, then your implementation procedures will become more effective. Ensure to keep your plan concise. Never make it too broad and complex that it becomes unattainable; rather, make it sustainable.

Your plan must guide all your actions; yet, it would also be a measure or a qualitative analysis by which you can determine whether your performances are failing or succeeding. Apparently, you never want setting yourself up for failure right from the start.

## Step 1 – Establish Your Social Media Marketing Objectives

**The first step to your plan is to create the goals, purposes or objectives of your business that you wish to achieve.** When you have these goals from the outset, they will enable you to react quickly whenever your campaign plan is not meeting your requirements and expectations. Without having them, you will never have any means of measuring your success or manifesting your ROI from using social media networks.

Each piece of your strategy caters to the goals you preset. **You cannot simply advance without knowing what you are working on.** Look closely at the overall needs of your business so you can decide properly how you want to apply your participation in social media networks towards contributing to attaining your goals.

**Undoubtedly, you will be coming up with so many personalized and business-oriented goals.** However, the fundamentally relevant goals that most businesses include in their campaign strategies are, retaining customers, heightening brand awareness, and as much as possible, reducing the costs of marketing.

Ideally, you must choose a couple of primary goals and another couple of secondary goals to concentrate on. When you have too many goals, it can be distracting until ending up achieving none.

Align your goals with the broader and deeper aspects of your plan. In this way, your social media marketing efforts will be driving towards your business objectives. When your social media marketing plan exhibits support to your business goals, you will have greater opportunities of receiving investments and executive buy-ins.

Determining what metrics you should use to gauge the performance of your plan's implementation is a vital component in setting effective goals. Skip those metrics that only measure vanity such as 'like' and 'retweets'. Concentrate on the more significant aspects of web referrals, generated leads, and conversion rates.

Always keep your target customers and audience in mind when writing down your goals. Create their personas or archetypes, which involve details and data about them (i.e., their interests, demographics, pain points, etc.) so you can also test your goals. For instance, when you are striving to determine whether you have provided enough and proper substance to your goals, you can ask yourself how these goals help you to reach your target audience.

More importantly, apply the S.M.A.R.T. business framework approach of setting up goals. Meaning, each of your goals must be *'Specific- Measurable-Attainable-Relevant-Time-bound.'*

For example, your S.M.A.R.T. goal might read as this: "For YouTube, the business will be sharing videos that communicate its brand and culture. Goal implementation is through posting three videos a week. Goal target for each post shall be 5 comments and 30 'likes,' at the least."

## Step 2 – Conduct a Comprehensive Survey and Audit of Your Current and Prospective Social Media Accounts

Before creating your social media campaign plan, you also need to evaluate first your present social media usage on the most relevant sites. Have a better understanding of how your participation in social media is working for you and your business.

The implications of these evaluations are to figure out who is connecting with you through social media at present; which among the social media platforms your target customers use more frequently; and, how your presence and activity in social media fares to those of your competitors'.

After conducting your comprehensive social media survey and audit, you should come out with a clearer picture of which social media accounts can ably represent your business, how to manage these accounts, and for what specific purpose each account serves. You should maintain this social media audit periodically, especially when you are still in the process of scaling your business.

In addition, it must also become apparent which of these social media accounts require updating, or even demand your deactivation. When your audit discovers fraudulent or fake accounts, report them immediately. Reporting these deceitful accounts will help you to ensure people searching for your business online will connect only with the official accounts you manage. This is an important stage where you can also build a growing relationship with your target customers, founded on trust and goodwill.

Social media auditing becomes the perfect phase of the process of assessing which platforms you wish to use continuously or add potentially to the mix. Review also the creation of your audience personas so you can also determine which social media sites will be most effective for your brand.

You only have to ask yourself a couple of questions upon deciding which social media channels you will be moving forward with— 'are my target customers present on this site... and, if so, how do they actually use the platform? If you are not sure who uses what and how, then check out the respective statistics (discussed in Chapter 6, Chapter 7, and Chapter 8) of these particular sites to address your questions.

Take note that it is much better to use optimally fewer social media outlets as opposed to stretching yourself thin by trying to maintain your activities and presence on all the major social media networks. Remember the S.M.A.R. T. approach; you must make your plan sustainable.

As an equally important component of your comprehensive social media audit, create your brand's mission statements for each of the social media outlets you are planning to use. **These single statement declarations will help you to concentrate more towards attaining specific goals in each of the networks you will be using. If your marketing efforts start to lag, then these principled statements will be guiding your actions and get you back on track.**

Take your sweet time in determining your principal purposes in every social media profile you have or will join. Now, if you cannot draw out its purpose, then it would probably be better for you to delete or deactivate altogether those concerned profiles.

A good example of a mission statement might read as this: 'The business will use Twitter to share the brighter and lighter side of the brand and link up with the younger set of prospective customers.'

As soon as you have done determining which social media outlets to use for your business, consider also to determine the voice, tone, and style of your brand. This may include certain stylized aspects such as the type of language (i.e., colloquial, formal, informal, conversational, etc.) to use for each account, files to post (i.e., photos, videos, GIFs, plain texts, etc.), and so on.

**Step 3 – Improve Your Social Media Profile Accounts: The Creation and Reinvention of Your Audience Persona**

Enhance your social media presence when you have already completed the auditing of your social media sites. Build up your social media profiles with your audience persona and broader goals in mind. Each social media platform has a unique set of people; thus, you should treat each of them differently.

Update your existing accounts, and refine them to attain satisfactory results. Optimizing your social media profiles for SEO will help you to generate more traffic to your properties online. Performing cross-promotions of social media accounts will certainly extend the reach of your posts or contents. Generally, you should fill out completely all your social media profiles. Optimize all your posts and contents (i.e., images, videos, texts, and other files).

## Step 4: Collate Social Media Marketing Inspirations

A common issue you may encounter in implementing your plan is being doubtful about what types of information and content will be generating the most active customer engagements. Get your marketing inspirations from looking at what others in your business industry are sharing and how they use their respective social media channels.

Doing so will let you distinguish yourself or your business from your competitors. At the same time, by observing them, this will give you the opportunity to appeal to prospective leads your competitors might be missing.

Do not discount your target audience since they can also present a myriad of social media inspirations. **These inspirations not only come from the contents they share but also, in how they communicate with their messages.** Observe how your target audiences compose their tweets or type down their status updates. Try to give your best mimicking their style. Be among them, and learn their habits. Apply these observations as bases to your social media campaign plan.

Another significant source of social media inspiration is the influencers and industry leaders. **A number of business moguls, celebrities, and giant companies perform excellently with their own social media campaigns.** Through advanced, creative, and innovative social media strategies, these social media stalwarts were able to distinguish themselves more prominently. You should follow them since you can learn so much from their styles.

The following are suggested references for your social media inspiration for each particular aspect of social media marketing:

➢ Digital Content Marketing Strategy – **Virgin, Unbounce**

➢ Facebook Systematic Schemes – **Walmart, Coca-Cola**

➢ Instagram Systematic Schemes – **General Electric, Herschel Supply Company**

➢ Twitter Systematic Schemes – **Oreo, Charmin**

➢ Social Media Advertising Strategy – **The American Red Cross, Airbnb**

➢ Social Media Customer Service Strategy – **Warby Parker, Tangerine Bank**

## Step 5: Create Your Social Media Content Marketing Plan

An essential part to succeed in your social media campaigns is having a great, unique, and high-quality content to share. Your social media content marketing plan should comprise your strategies for creating such contents, curating them, as well as using a content calendar for scheduling their ideal posting times.

Social media and contents exist within a complemental relationship. Social media without great content is useless, and conversely, content without social media lets nobody know about you or your business. Hence, you ought to use them both together to reach your prospects and eventually make a conversion.

Nevertheless, you must first answer the following questions in order for you to create your social media content marketing strategy:

➢ What should be the types of content intended for posting and promoting on social media?

➢ Who will be the target audiences receiving each type of content?

➢ What should be the appropriate frequency for posting the content?

➢ Who will be creating the content?

➢ How will the business promote the content?

For a satisfactory social media content strategy, it combines a triumvirate of important components: content type, posting time, posting frequency.

The typical contents you should post on each platform rely on context and form. The context suits the voice of your business and the trending contents within the particular platform (i.e., serious, funny, informative, etc.) The form is the way you present your contextual contents— links, images, videos, plain text, etc.

Specific times for posting on each site depend on several available statistics and studies on these sites. However, never treat these studies as hard rules, but rather apply them as your guidelines when to post your contents to achieve a much higher engagement. Bear in mind that you always have a unique target audience; thus, you should test and evaluate the ideal posting time for yourself.

The intention of the frequency of sharing your contents is not to annoy or bore your target audience. Figuring out the best posting frequency is crucial since it could only mean either two things: more unfollows/unlikes or more engagements with your posted/uploaded content. You may check out Facebook Insights so you will take note on when your followers are present online or engage with your content.

## Step 6: Allocate Your Budget and Resources

Budgeting for your social media marketing efforts would be looking into the corresponding tactics you have chosen to achieve your goals. Therefore, you should create first a comprehensive list of the apps or tools you may need (i.e., email marketing, social media monitoring, and customer relationship management).

Include also in your list the various services you may want to outsource (i.e., video production, graphic design, content writing, etc.), as well as any forms of advertising you may need to purchase. Following each entry, include also the annual estimated cost of your plan in order for you to have a clearer picture of what you are investing in and the ways it would influence your social media marketing plan budget.

Several businesses set initially their budget, and then, choose from among the strategies that fit the set budget. However, you can take the reverse approach, establishing a social media campaign strategy first prior to determining or setting the budget that suits the chosen strategy.

Now, if the expenses of executing your strategy exceed your estimated budget, then you need to prioritize your strategies in accordance with their respective ROI schedules. Your chosen strategies that entail the fastest ROI (usually, social media referrals and advertising purchases) must be your primary priorities since these tactics generate immediate profits, which you may eventually invest into long-term strategies (i.e., the creation of quality contents, acquisition of fans, or engagements over the long haul).

## Step 7: Test, Evaluate, and Adjust Your Strategy

Always rely on periodic testing procedures so you can figure out what necessary adjustments you may need for your social media marketing strategy plan. Try to create testing capabilities for each marketing effort you will be taking on the various social media platforms you are using. For instance, you might want to:

➢ Monitor the number of clicks that your links receive on a certain channel. Use URL shortener services and urchin tracking module (UTM) parameters for your links. UTM parameters are five versions of URL parameters marketers often use to monitor and measure the effectiveness of their online campaigns across publishing media and traffic sources.

➢ Use the social media analytics by Hootsuite to monitor the reach and success of your campaigns.

➢ Use Google Analytics to track the number of page visits of your website/weblog or its traffic driven by your social media accounts.

➢ Keep a log of each of your successes and failures and analyze them individually. By doing so, you can make the necessary adjustments to your social media marketing strategy plan.

➢ Conduct surveys, both online and offline. These appraisal activities are great ways for gauging your marketing success. You may source respondents from your email list or the base of your website visitors and social media followers, and ask them how you are performing on social media.

Such direct approaches are oftentimes very effective. Subsequently, you may also ask your offline prospects and customers whether social media has made a big influence on their purchasing.

These insights might just prove to be priceless, especially when you look at certain areas of your plan where you can improve. For all you know, the most important aspect for you to understand concerning your social media campaign strategy plan is that it must be evolving continuously with the changing times and trends.

With the emergence of new social media networks, you may have certain reasons to include them in your plan. While being able to achieve certain goals, you will have to set again new targets.

There will always be unexpected challenges and unpredictable issues arising along your way; you just simply need to address them. While scaling your business, you may also need to add and reinvent new roles or develop your presence on social media to the different regions or branches of your business.

Rewrite to improve and benchmark your social media marketing strategy plan. Ensure that these proposed improvements reflect the latest insights of your business, as well as those from the social media community. Additionally, always see to it that your social media marketing team is aware of all the updates of your plan.

> *"Start with the soul and end with the sale. Not the other way around."*
>
> — **CC Chapman**

## Social Media Is the Internet: A Conclusion

Overall, social media marketing is extremely a potent marketing tool. Not all business enterprises have yet known and understood how to apply properly social media in their respective lines of businesses.

Many skeptics still believe the application of social media for business is like treading across an unknown and unchartered territory. On the contrary, the ever-growing disciples of social media marketing only need to implement social media marketing plans for business through a stable and strongly defined strategy.

The few entailing risks and limitations related to social media marketing may seem to be scary, if not, challenging. Nevertheless, they only become precautions for marketers to take over time to achieve success in their social media strategies.

This handbook has analyzed closely the realm of social media marketing. It has detailed the principal business benefits and defined the various leading types of social media platforms with their respective roles. Truly, whether a business enterprise develops its presence on every social media channel, or perhaps, only on a couple of selected ones, the benefits vary in terms of volume and value.

Nonetheless, the principal benefits usually gained are heightened brand exposure and business reputation management, SEO and increased traffic, word-of-mouth promotion and lead generation, market and competitor insights associated to the target audience, and facilities for human resource and public relations.

Furthermore, although social media marketing is essentially a cost-effective solution, it generally depends on which specific type of social media channels that marketers use.

Aside from the leading blogs and microblogs, social media networks, and photo/video-sharing sites, social media professionals also consider social bookmarking sites, social events sites, wikis, and forums as social media platforms. Each of these social media outlets can all become significantly beneficial for business enterprises in their own way.

Concerning the imminent outsourcing of social media marketing teams, it is more prudent to believe that a lean in-house internal social presence is far more profitable compared to a huge outsourced counterpart. Besides, the ROI of using social media is definitely about insights and experience instead of the number of fans.

Business enterprises nowadays are already catching up and starting to use social media marketing. They test various social media marketing tactics and measure their results; yet, their social media presence is still just about to fully bloom. While the beginning of the new decade (2010 to 2020) is usually about establishing a solid fan base and building networks, the middle part is certainly about the objectives of achieving customer engagement, building customer trust, goodwill, and relationships, and encouraging nurturing customer loyalty.

**One cannot yet conclude the entire successes of social media strategies. The changing times bring forth new opportunities each day within the realm of social media. Each platform evolves constantly, presenting significant marketing aspects for business.**

In addition, each month sees a new launch of social media platforms, which offer novel business potentials and new sections of marketing research. Hence social media marketing remains a work in progress.

Moreover, mobile marketing is beginning to change the future and landscape of social media marketing. Now that the Internet is easily available and accessible on smartphones, social media users can access their emails anywhere, anytime— and more than they usually do so.

As mobile devices have been opening more and more emails, email marketing will indeed be having a rebirth. The question posing amidst everyone now is how shall a business enterprise combine altogether mobile marketing, social media marketing, and email marketing?

Concerning the usage and preference of social media sites, not much has actually altered. Truth is the world is just simply witnessing an amplification of current social media trends:

At present, the smartphone is undisputedly the chief liaison and delivery device for online services and content creation. Hence, if you want to participate on social media, you need to participate on mobile.

In the world of social media, visual contents rule. This is actually a direct consequence of the high emergence of using smartphones. Add to the fact is the current tendency of social media users to publish much less in favor of a simple reading consumption.

**As a full-pledged marketer or advertiser, you always have to make everything easier and more convenient for your target audience. Thus, you only have to rely more on posting or uploading visual contents (i.e., videos, photos, infographics, etc.) and organic ads (i.e., emoji and branded stickers).**

Indeed, online social media commerce is forever here to stay. Regardless if it is to inspire or nurture qualified prospects for your physical point-of-sale outlet or e-commerce website, all of the important social media apps/tools that you may need to empower current customers or stimulate their purchasing behavior can be accessible from the major social media outlets.

Therefore, it is now all up to you to design and charter your social media marketing destiny while avoiding the pits of saturation.

*"If TV is still catching the last of its breaths, then undoubtedly, it has lost its former lofty position of being a legendary leader as a media. Amidst a large, new conglomerate, social media remains to pose as the new kid on the block— whether it is on top of the communication tunnel (hosting, storing, sharing, and sourcing of contents); right at the bottom of the purchasing funnel (sales and distribution); or, in the middle (communication, interaction, and brand management). Social media is, indeed, the new Internet. Social media is, indeed, the new media."*

— **Roger Burns**

www.ingramcontent.com/pod-product-compliance
Lightning Source LLC
Chambersburg PA
CBHW052249220526
45471CB00001B/263